World vs. Bob Chisholm

World vs. Bob Chisholm
Surviving Small Town Radio

Candy Chisholm Justice
and
Bryan Cottingham

Copyright © 2024 Candace Justice and Bryan Cottingham.

Cover photo: courtesy Bain Hughes.

ISBN: 979-8-9893644-5-9

All rights reserved.

"City of New Orleans"
Words and music by Steve Goodman
Copyright © 1970 Sony Music Publishing (US) LLC
Copyright renewed
All rights administered by Sony Music Publishing (US) LLC 424 Church Street, Suite 1200, Nashville, TN 37219.
International copyright secured. All rights reserved.
Reprinted by permission of Hal Leonard LLC

WARNING: Unauthorized duplication or downloading is a violation of applicable laws. File sharing is allowed only with those companies with which Publisher James L. Dickerson or Sartoris Literary Group has a written agreement.

Sartoris Literary Group, Inc.
Metro-Jackson, Mississippi

DEDICATION

For my parents, Bob and Carol Chisholm, who taught me all I know about love, courage and laughter

—Candy Chisholm Justice.

To the people and town of Winona, Mississippi, the place where it all started, and the place to where it always returns. To Bob, my mentor, my inspiration, and my dear friend. And to the ghosts of the announcers and journalists who roam the control rooms and newsrooms of today, watching over and guiding those who came later. May we all live up to their legacies.

—Bryan Cottingham.

CONTENTS

Prologue ……………………………………………... (i)

Chapter 1: The Police Did What? …………………… 17

Chapter 2: Imaginary Big Brothers …………………. 33

Chapter 3: The Killer Sheriff ………………………. 69

Chapter 4: Antics and Pranks ……………………… 93

Chapter 5: Fannie Lou Hamer ……………………... 125

Chapter 6: The Bad Guys Almost Win ……………... 135

Chapter 7: Dr. Martin Luther King ………………… 143

Chapter 8: Desegregation Comes to Winona …. ……. 155

Chapter 9: Candy's Life of Crime ………………….. 167

Chapter 10: That Memphis *Thang* .. ……….……….. 203

Chapter 11: Epilogue ……………………………….. 211

More from the Authors ………………………….…. 227

Acknowledgements ……………………………….. 282

Radio Glossary ………………………………….…. 284

PROLOGUE

> "When you hear it, it is news.
> When you read it, it is history."
> —Bob Chisholm's favorite radio quote—

Saturday, October 25, 1958.

Winona, Miss.—It was early fall, and the town was about to change. Residents had been puzzled and intrigued for weeks by chalk stencils on the sidewalks and streets that mysteriously declared "WONA is coming." But what, exactly, was a "wona?" People wanted to know. Anybody inside the second floor of the Telephone Building in downtown Winona that fall morning knew exactly what WONA was: The call letters of the town's first—and still only—radio station licensed to broadcast from sunup to sundown..

Winona was a microcosm of small-town Mississippi life in 1958. Mississippi was among the first states, along with Alabama and Georgia, to reject ratification of the 19th Amendment that guaranteed women the right to vote—and it was the last state to ratify the amendment in 1984. Of course, after the amendment was ratified nationwide in 1920 and became the law of the land, women in Mississippi were entitled to vote; but to do so they had to choose between one of two options: they could either file a lawsuit in federal court or they could convince the voting registrar in their county to obey the constitution and register them. Sadly, few women had the family or marital support to do either.

Among the first to take the leap was Miss Belle Kearney, the unmarried daughter of plantation owners in Madison County, a nationally known supporter of women's suffrage, and the author of two books. Her father was a First Lt. Colonel in the 18th Mississippi Regiment and fought at Vicksburg. Throughout her life she either lived with her parents or, when they died, her brother and his family. Well known as a rebel on social issues, she announced her intention to run for the state senate three months after the 19th Amendment was ratified and two years later went on to become Mississippi's first female state senator. It was the seat that had been held by her father, so there may have been a sympathy vote involved. Looking back on her very unusual-for-the-times lifestyle, she was the first non-traditional female ever elected to the state senate and, if so, she was certainly not the last. Irony has always been one of Mississippi's most valuable assets.

Black, Asian, Hispanic, and Native American residents, although granted the constitutional right, effectively could not vote because of state and local restrictions until passage of the Civil Rights Act of 1965. Voting was only one of the issues that held back women and non-whites. In 1958 schools, restaurants, and public buildings were strictly separated by race. Waiting rooms, restrooms and drinking fountains were prominently marked for use by "White" or "Colored" only. Women were a decade and a half away from even getting a credit card without their husband's approval and signature. Girls graduating from high school could only look to a future as a housewife, a secretary, a nurse, or a teacher.

Residents could not make a local phone call without going through a nosy operator who could listen to every word spoken. Many people did not have televisions, so they had to watch comic superstars Milton Berle and Lucille Ball from lawn chairs on the sidewalk outside a furniture store. Most families did not have washers and clothes dryers, and air conditioners in homes were a rarity. Although nobody realized it at the time, drastic changes were coming to Winona and to the entire country.

In the midst of this economic, social and democratic malaise, a 28-year-old man named Bob Chisholm quietly brought his wife and young daughter to the small town to start and manage a fledging radio station. He wasn't quiet for long. Residents soon realized he was different from almost every other radio station manager in the state. Bob Chisholm dragged Winona — sometimes kicking and screaming — to a place that was new and daring!

Excited people of every age crowded into the tiny radio studio to hear Station Manager Bob Chisholm, put WONA on the air with these words:

> **Good morning. This is radio station WONA in Winona, Mississippi, with studios in the Telephone Building. WONA operates on an assigned frequency of 1570 kilocycles with an operating power of one thousand watts as authorized by the Federal Communications Commission, Washington, D.C....We invite you to stay tuned to WONA all day long for music, the latest world and local news, programs from the Mutual Broadcasting System, sports and special events.**

Though Chisholm did not mention it specifically that first day, his 7 a.m. Morning Edition of the News would soon draw nearly every Winonian to the radio while they ate breakfast every morning. Bob wore many hats at WONA but was first and foremost a dedicated journalist. He and his wife Carol would go on to win many awards for their outstanding news and feature reporting.

On the day Bob Chisholm launched WONA, among those crowded into the studio were their 6-year-old daughter Candy and 12-year-old Bryan Cottingham, who lived with his parents and younger brothers on Webster Street, where the Chisholm family also lived. Candy was nonchalant. After all, this was just her Daddy doing what her Daddy always did. He was talking on the radio. It wasn't until a few years later when she picked up the phone and heard a stranger snarl, "I'm going to kill your Daddy!" that she began to understand the significance of that first morning broadcast.

Throughout those early years, Candy saw the good, the bad and the ugly associated with taking stands on emotional issues and reporting news that was sometimes painful for local residents to hear. It was due to her parents' unwavering devotion to their profession and their support of her ambitions that she grew up to become a journalist who shared her parents' professional values.

Bryan was in awe. The announcers were gods in his mind. They were playing records and talking on the radio! He ran home after the broadcast and breathlessly told his parents he was going to be a radio announcer when he grew up. For the next three years, he hung around the radio station every chance he got. Bryan swept the floors, got Cokes and sandwiches for the announcers, and filed record albums after they were played — a chore the announcers hated. Eventually, they started letting him select and pull records at the beginning of their shifts. He learned how to operate the "control board" that brought all the elements of a program together.

Bob recognized Bryan's zeal, encouraged his questions and always seemed to have the time to introduce something new. When Bryan was 15, Bob offered him a part-time job as an announcer. At that moment, the young boy realized he had just ascended Olympus. The view was breathtaking.

Over the years, Bob became much more than a boss. He was a mentor, a guide, and eventually a dear friend. Bryan learned so much more from him than just how to talk on the radio. Bob showed him the value of preparation, the absolute necessity of integrity, and the overwhelming satisfaction of doing a job well. He prodded, encouraged, and gently corrected, always treating Bryan as a professional. He taught him never to let anyone else work harder than he did. And then Bob *always* worked harder than Bryan did. That was Bob Chisholm.

This book chronicles the impact of local radio on small Southern towns in the 1950s and 1960s and the impact of these towns on local radio at a time when rock 'n' roll was spawning a social revolution in American culture. Central to this account is a story of journalistic integrity, hard work, and dedication to a craft.

The title of this memoir comes from one of Bob's favorite stories. Radio broadcasters must deal with the FCC (Federal Communications Commission) and music corporations such as ASCAP and BMI, which collect royalties for songwriters and entertainers. This can sometimes make life miserable for radio management and on-the-air people.

A lesser-known music publisher, World Music, once filed a frivolous lawsuit against hundreds of small radio stations and when the formal papers arrived on Bob's desk, he burst into laughter when he saw across the top: "World vs. Bob Chisholm." In a very real sense, there were many times during his life in Winona that it must have felt like everybody really was out to get him, so Bob took great delight in showing people the lawsuit to prove that he had not been imagining that the whole world *really* was against him.

Candy Chisholm Justice
Bryan Cottingham

Winona, Mississippi
Population, 4,282

Bob Chisholm, general manager WONA   Chisholm family photo.

Chapter 1

The Police Did What?

"If you do one more bad story on the radio about the police department, the mayor or the Board of Aldermen, we're going to beat you within an inch of your life."

It was four o'clock in the morning, and WONA radio station manager Bob Chisholm was startled to find the entire city police force (all five of them) waiting for him at the ground-floor front door of the Telephone Building in downtown Winona, Mississippi. He had arrived at his usual time to prepare The Morning Edition of the News. His 7 a.m. daily 15-minute newscast was how the residents of Winona (population 4,282) kept up with everything that was happening in their town—from births and funerals to church and school events to what was going on in City Hall. It was must-listen radio in the fifties and sixties.

Many people in Winona government did not like Bob. They would almost always get upset when he aired his regular report from City Hall on the Morning Edition. Quite often, the report carried information city officials would rather not have the public know. From time to time, Bob would get threats, some veiled and others overt, or muttered comments about his reports. This morning, the threats were very real and very frightening.

It was sometime during the summer before Bryan's senior year in high school. He was not usually an early riser, but he wanted to be at the station to watch while Bob prepared the news and delivered the Morning Edition. When Bryan got to the station around 5:45

a.m., he walked upstairs and tried to open the door to go inside. The door was locked. This was unusual because Bob never locked the door. No one in town locked their doors in those days. Bryan knocked on the glass and was surprised to see Bob furtively looking around the corner to see who was there. When he saw Bryan, he hurried to the door, quickly unlocked it and let him in. Just as quickly, Bob relocked the door and hurried Bryan back into his office. The first thing Bob said was, "Did you see anyone else downstairs when you came in?" Bryan was puzzled. Something wasn't right. After Bryan assured Bob no one was waiting when he came up, Bob told him an incredible story.

The night before, Bob had attended a meeting of the Mayor and Board of Aldermen where the police force had been given what Bob felt was an undeserved raise, their third in the last few months. The board members must have been uncomfortable about the increase because they had warned Bob that he better not say anything about it on the news. You didn't tell Bob Chisholm not to put something newsworthy on the air.

Bob told him about his early morning confrontation with the police, and their threat to beat him within an inch of his life. Sixty years later, Bryan still remembers the chilling effect those words had on him. His mentor and friend had just had his life threatened. Bob told him he was going to air the story and that Bryan should go home right away because he wasn't sure what the police would do when he reported the warning on the air.

Without hesitation, Bryan told him he wanted to stay and help. The foolishness of youth is sometimes wonderfully blind. Bob realized that, even if they did something to him, they would never hurt a 16-year-old kid. He agreed to let Bryan stay but told him to keep away from the windows while he finished writing the story.

WONA was located on the second floor of the two-story building on the right. Photo courtesy Candy Chisholm Justice.

A word about the layout of the station. It was located upstairs in the Telephone Building on the corner of Summit and Front Streets in downtown Winona. There was a door with a glass window at the entrance to the bottom of the stairs that led to a room where the telephone operators worked and to the entrance lobby of WONA. The upstairs door also had a glass window that gave a clear view of the glassed-in control room.

Anyone standing at the lobby door could clearly see whoever was in the control room. Another windowed door gave a clear view of the separate studio from which Bob usually delivered the news. Not a very good situation when armed policemen were unhappy with you.

Bob finished writing his story about 6:15. The two of them sat on the floor under the control console while Bob recorded his dispassionate, but firm delivery of the story. Bryan remembers the opening line: "Stay tuned for a story about the most blatant case of official police intimidation you have ever heard."

Bob continued his report, detailing the entire incident. He ended the story vowing to keep reporting the news as it happened and assured listeners he would never be bullied into doing otherwise. The report was stunning.

Soon after Bob finished recording the story, Bryan signed the station on the air. To make sure he was safe, Bryan sat on the floor below the eye-line of the control room window as he played records and read commercials. Bryan was so caught up in the events, he never took time to comprehend how surreal the moment was. As the time for the news approached, Bob was on the phone with E.W. "Pop" Wages, the county sheriff and one of Bob's friends and supporters. Bob had called him earlier to report the incident, and Wages said he would keep driving by the front door to make sure no one tried to come in.

Seven o'clock came and Bryan read the opening to The Morning Edition of the News. Usually, the news was reported live, but this time, Bob wanted to make sure everything was presented exactly right, so Bryan hit the "play" button on the Norelco tape recorder above his head. The story began. Bob and Bryan scooted farther under the control panel and waited, listening to the story but listening even more closely for the sound of breaking glass and the door opening. That was the only time Bryan remembers feeling afraid. The impact of what was happening finally hit him.

The phone started ringing immediately. Bob let it ring until after the story was finished. When it was over, and nothing had happened, they both breathed a little easier. Sheriff Wages came upstairs to make sure everything was okay and made periodic checks during the rest of the day. Bob and Bryan started answering the phone. There were a number of calls supporting Bob, many expressing outrage at what had happened. There were, of course, a few calls telling Bob he would have gotten what he deserved. That was to be expected. Miraculously, everything seemed to die down by the end of the day, and they thought everything was over. It wasn't.

Cops Exact Their Revenge

Weeks passed. Bob's family didn't dare hope that the Winona Police had given up on seeking revenge against Bob. But then again maybe they *had* given up. Maybe they wouldn't dare try to hurt Bob when Sheriff Wages, a good law enforcement officer and a good friend, was on to them.

Maybe they would not be brazen enough to beat Bob Chisholm "within an inch of his life" after the whole town had heard about the threat on the 7 a.m. news on WONA. Maybe. They didn't openly talk about *why*, but Bob started calling Carol before he left the station to come home if it was after dark. He did it on the pretense, for Candy's sake, that he was letting Carol know she could go ahead and put supper on the table.

So the Chisholms started to feel that after all this time, it was less likely that the police would do anything to hurt them. The station was just about three blocks from their house, and because Bob got to work so early every day, he always got to park right in front of the radio station. It was dark, so the call came from Bob that he was leaving to come home, a trip that usually took less than five minutes. Every night Carol and Candy held their collective breath until he arrived safely home. But on this night, five minutes

Bob at the WONA control board.
Photo courtesy Candy Chisholm Justice

passed, and he did not walk through the door. Carol and Candy looked at each other, refusing to panic until a few more minutes had passed. Carol called the station hoping he had gotten tied up with some unexpected work. No answer.

Carol and Candy just stood there looking at the front door, willing it to open. Finally, the door did open, but Candy's usual smiling daddy did not come through the door. Instead, her father — bloodied, with broken eyeglasses and clothes ripped — fell face down onto the living room floor. Candy ran into the bedroom crying and screaming, "My daddy is dead! They killed my daddy!" while her mother grabbed a Coke bottle that was nearby and headed out the door to exact her own revenge on whoever had hurt her husband.

Hearing his daughter's screams, Bob dragged himself up off the floor and stumbled after Candy, saying, "I'm okay, Baby. I'm not dead." Carol, not finding anyone to hit over the head with the Coke bottle, came back inside and put her arms around her husband and daughter, and they all sat down on the sofa so he could tell them exactly what had happened. They assumed he would say it was the police who had beat him up, but instead he said it was a man who had worked at the radio station years before, whom Bob had fired.

Candy and Carol were confused, but Bob quickly cleared it up. The Winona police had hired the guy to beat up Bob, and they told him to make it abundantly clear that they were behind the attack. With every fist hurled into Bob's face and stomach, the man said the name of one of the policemen until they had all been represented by a fist or two.

Then without even a bandage or a glass of water, Bob scrambled around to find his extra eyeglasses, called Sheriff Wages and then drove himself to the home of the Justice of the Peace to swear out an assault warrant against the assailant and the policemen.

Weeks passed again. Bob walked from the radio station to the nearby City Café for his usual morning coffee break. Inside, he found all the Winona policemen drinking coffee with the man they had hired to beat up Bob, all of them smiling smugly. The message was clear: You can swear out all the warrants you want to, Chisholm, but nobody on the Winona police force is going to arrest the guy who beat you up.

··········

Years after the Chisholm family had moved away from Winona, Bob was shocked when one of those Winona policemen walked into his new office. It was Bill Surrell, who had driven to Memphis to ask for Bob's forgiveness. Surrell, a sworn enemy of

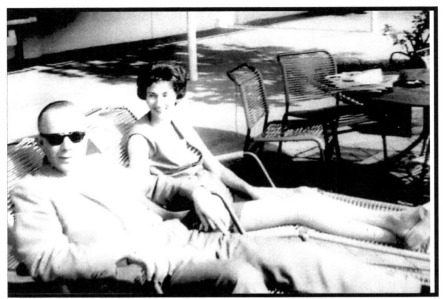

Bob and Carol at the swimming pool at the Edgewater Gulf Hotel in Biloxi, Mississippi during Mississippi Broadcasters Association meeting. Photo courtesy Candy Chisholm.

enemy of Bob's in Winona, told Bob that he had recently become a Christian and was deeply ashamed of his part in the beating that had been delivered in front of their house. He said he wouldn't blame Bob if he wasn't willing to forgive.

But Bob also had become a Christian in the intervening years, so he told Bill Surrell that he accepted the apology, and the two men shook hands and embraced. Bob had tears in his eyes when he told Carol and Candy about Bill's visit.

Everyone was really shocked that Surrell had apologized, but all the bad feelings of the past seemed less important after that handshake and embrace. It must be said, however, that if Bill Surrell and the thug the police had hired, had killed Bob or injured him seriously, it is doubtful that either Carol or Candy could have forgiven the contrite officer.

Bob and Carol and Candy

Bob and Carol had been bitten by the radio bug in the late 1940s and each dropped out of college to pursue the exciting life of radio careers. It would never have occurred to them back then that the glamorous radio life would also sometimes be fraught with danger.

They both considered Demopolis, Alabama, their hometown, but because their families lived there at different times, just barely overlapping, Bob and Carol didn't really know each other until they both went to work at the Demopolis radio station WXAL, which they always called Waxal. Carol had loved majoring in art at Auburn University and had lots of friends there, so dropping out was a hard decision. But for Bob, leaving Transylvania University in Lexington, Kentucky, to go to radio school in Minneapolis was an easy choice.

To support himself there, Bob worked as a waiter in a nightclub, and he always loved telling stories about the big-tipping shady characters who hung out there. In radio school, he learned how to operate a radio station control board and other necessary skills, but most importantly, he developed a velvety smooth radio voice that did not betray his southern upbringing. A radio announcer, he always said, should not have any kind of regional accent to distract from what the announcer is saying.

Bob and Carol fell in love quickly while working at Waxal. Bob's parents by then lived in Tupelo, Mississippi, but Carol lived with her parents in Demopolis, and Bob walked her home after work every day and was usually invited to stay for supper. When Bob got a better job offer at a radio station in another Alabama town, he took it, but since the station was powerful enough to be heard in Demopolis — during on-air shifts, he played records of love songs for Carol, who listened to him every night. One of their favorites was "I'd Like to Get You on a Slow Boat to China, All to Myself Alone…" Another favorite was "P.S. I Love You," which was about a couple separated by war.

When Bob proposed, Carol's parents, Walton and Ada Burkett, gave the young couple a choice: a big wedding like Carol's sister Jane had had when she married her high school sweetheart Austin Caldwell, or they could have the money a big wedding would have cost, which they could use to start their married life. They made the practical choice and got married in a small family ceremony and moved to Bob's first big-city radio job in Montgomery, Alabama. Late in her life, Carol told her daughter she always regretted not having a big wedding like her sister had, but she never regretted marrying her sweetheart Bob.

Even with the generous wedding gift of money from Carol's parents, Bob and Carol didn't have a car and money was tight, so on their first married Christmas, they walked to a Christmas tree lot in Montgomery and bought a small tree for their apartment. When they put it up, Bob just hated it. It was too small, he said, — a Christmas tree should touch the ceiling. So they gave the tree away and went back for a taller tree, and Bob created a big silver star for the top made from cardboard covered with aluminum foil with part of a coat hanger to hold it to the top of the tree.

Wherever they moved, that star went with them, and for the rest of their lives, Bob and Carol always had that star on the top of their tree. It is now on the top of their daughter's Christmas tree every year — 70 years and counting. The aluminum foil has to be replaced every 10 years or so, but it is the same cardboard base that Bob carefully designed in 1949.

Later, in Winona, Bob and Carol lived in a rental house with 13-foot ceilings, and Bob always insisted their fresh-cut Christmas tree had to touch the ceiling. Bob, who was both a traditionalist and somebody who found new things interesting and exciting, in the 1960s brought home one of those tacky silver artificial trees that were all the rage at that time.

Carol took one look at the silver Christmas tree and said, "Bob, have you lost your mind?" The aluminum tree lasted a few hours, and then Bob went out and cut down their traditional 13-foot fresh-cut cedar tree from a friend's farm. The aluminum tree went to the radio station studio.

••••••••••

Bob and Carol's only child, Candy, was born on February 2, 1951, while her parents still lived in Montgomery. A friend with a car took them to the hospital when Carol went into labor, and after the baby was born and Carol woke up from the anesthesia, she told Bob she was sorry he didn't get the baby boy he had been counting on, but Bob insisted then and the rest of his life that he had never wanted a son, that a girl was what he had wanted all along.

Bob had to rush off to the Montgomery radio station to work his double shift soon after Candy was born. Oddly enough for the South, Candy's birth came during a huge snow and ice storm that had toppled telephone poles and trees and made communication with the outside world nearly impossible.

Bob, of course, was anxious to let his parents in Tupelo, Mississippi, know their first grandchild had been born and that the baby was a girl, so he tried to put a letter on the train, but the storm was so bad that the trains were not running on time and the letter would not arrive until the next day. So then he contacted a ham-radio operator, hoping he could get word to the new grandparents, but no luck.

The Montgomery radio station where Bob worked was powerful enough to be heard in parts of Mississippi, so Bob's father, Robert Alvin (Chiz) Chisholm, listened to his son's nightly "record show." A few years later, such shows were hosted by gregarious announcers who could play dedications and make personal comments on the air, but announcers in the early 50s had strict instructions to only announce song titles and musical artists and, of course, give station identifications.

Nothing personal was to be said on the air. But the announcers did get to select their own records to play on the air, and Bob chose to play the Mills Brothers singing "Daddy's Little Girl." Bob hoped his dad would catch the subtle message, and he did. "Grace!" Candy's excited grandfather shouted to his wife in the kitchen, "we've got a granddaughter!"

The fact that the baby was a girl was especially welcomed news since Grace and Chiz had raised three rambunctious, well-loved boys (Bob, Jack and Bill) but always grieved the death of their daughter, Mary Grace, who died when she was six months old. At last, there was a little girl in the family again!

What could be more appropriate than Candy's birth being announced on the radio (even if it was announced in code)! It was just the beginning of her childhood and adolescence in a radio family. When the family moved to Winona seven years later, Carol went back to working at a radio station with her husband. She hosted a weekday midday radio program called *Mainly for Women*, which would go on to win numerous awards from the Mississippi Broadcasters Association. She was most proud that her program won in the best show category, not the best *women's* show category.

Candy pretends she is a DJ.   Family photo.

Mainly for Women was a two-hour show that combined music and interesting features that Carol selected from the United Press International wire service that the station subscribed to. The features ranged from news like Jackie Kennedy's little black dress and pillbox hats, which was mainly of interest to women, to features that anybody could find interesting or get a laugh from.

FLASHBACK: CANDY JUSTICE

We had a big reel-to-reel tape recorder in our house that Mama used to record all the talk segments for "Mainly for Women." She would record the segments and then take the reel to the radio station, where the announcer on duty would integrate the music into the

Bob Chisholm, far right, and Carol, far left, met at this radio production in Alabama and subsequently married. Chisholm family photo.

program between feature segments.

That went smoothly when I was in school, but during the summer, my friends and I — banished from the house while Mama was recording her show — would get carried away playing in the yard and inevitably scream and make other loud noises that ruined whatever Mama was recording. So she would have to start over.

She was amazingly tolerant of our noisy slip-ups, but sometimes we interrupted her recording so often that she would barely get the program finished in time to drive quickly to the radio station, where Daddy would be waiting at the curb to grab the reel and rush it upstairs to the control room.

My mother had her own version of the velvet-smooth professional radio voice, but she didn't try to entirely eliminate her soft Southern accent. Her great voice and the fact that she was something of a local radio celebrity, got her invited to emcee all kinds of events — fashion shows, talent contests and Christmas programs that called for a professional narration of some kind.

She found a story in a magazine, called *The Night Mrs. Santa Claus Saved Christmas,* and that became her trademark. Every Christmas some club or other group would invite her to present her reading, and she also read it during *Mainly for Women* a few days before Christmas every year.

Montgomery County courthouse in Winona.
Mississippi Department of History and Archives.
Used by permission.

Chapter 2

Imaginary Big Brothers

Because Candy was an only child, it was entirely predictable that she would pretend that some of her dad's young disc jockeys were her big brothers. She never tried to claim Bryan or other announcers who were from Winona, because in a small town anyone would know that they were *not* her brothers.

However, when Bob hired a handsome college boy from Mississippi State University, Bill White, to work weekends, and he arrived in Winona driving a very cool sports car, it was too much to pass up. So Candy told the kids on Webster Street that Bill was her big brother, who came home on weekends and worked at their dad's radio station.

It was quite believable considering Bill often ate dinner with the Chisholm family during those weekends. Candy's friends were very impressed — so impressed, in fact, that they went home and told their parents about the Chisholms' college-aged son, Bill. And then their parents mentioned the "son" to Carol, and the charade was over. But Candy doesn't remember being particularly embarrassed by her lie being found out — 8-year-old kids just shrug off stuff like that, especially when the kid knows it's her parents' fault for not producing a *real* big brother for her.

Although she no longer lied about the cool announcers being her brothers, that doesn't mean she didn't privately pretend they were her siblings. Some of the announcers like Les Nabors were married and therefore never had dinner with the Chisholm family, or they were young enough to live with their own parents, as Bryan did in his early WONA years.

So it was only the slightly older, single guys who really did in many ways function as big brothers in Candy's life. One of them was Bobby Evans, whose father Bob Evans Sr. owned WONA, even though Mr. Evans lived in Tupelo, Mississippi. Candy never asked, but it's possible that her dad only hired Bobby because he was the boss's son. However, much to Bobby's credit, he never ever used his dad as leverage. He wanted to learn everything he could about the radio business from Bob. He was often asked to dinner by Bob and Carol, who genuinely liked Bobby. Candy thought he was a lot of fun to be around. He would eventually go on to manage and then own a radio station in Grenada, Mississippi.

When Bobby died in January of 2022 at the age of 81, his family put in his obituary: "After a short stint at the University of Southern Mississippi, he received a free ride to Winona from his father, who found out he had been present at Pat O'Brien's in New Orleans more than he had been in the classroom. He was put to work at his father's radio station (WONA) as the understudy of the infamous Bob Chisholm."

Bob would have gotten a great laugh out of being described as the "infamous Bob Chisholm."

A few years later, Van Jolly went to work as a WONA announcer, and Candy thought he was very hip. He did some promotions for the station that involved helping kids from the local high school raise money for charities like St. Jude Children's Research Hospital in Memphis, and he raised Candy's standing among her peers in the process. Years later, Van and the Chisholm family ended up living in Memphis and saw each other from time to time. It was always fun to see him.

Of all the young men who worked with Bob at WONA, the one who had the longest, closest relationship with him was Bryan, the co-author of this memoir. But the one who was closest to a big brother to Candy was Ed Forsythe. Ed never intended to make radio his long-term career, but he did love working at the station off and on until he settled into his own insurance business and got married.

Candy adored Ed, and he really was like a member of the family. He regularly ate dinner at their house and was always welcome there. He did all kinds of family things with them like decorating their 13-foot Christmas tree. Ed was a student at Ole Miss where he always seemed to be one or two classes shy of graduating. He was the drummer in the popular band The Downbeats and sometimes brought to the Chisholm house fellow band members or other Ole Miss friends — Candy always remembered one handsome college boy in particular.

FLASHBACK: CANDY JUSTICE

During the Vietnam War, Ed joined the Mississippi Air National Guard, which required him to spend several months in basic training in some other part of Mississippi. He asked my parents if he could leave his stereo system and extensive record collection with them while he was gone.

When he set up the stereo in our living room, he pulled out one album in particular and told them about a girl at Ole Miss breaking up with him and how he had gotten drunk that night and listened to that record over and over. I, who was about 12 and had never had a boyfriend, thought Ed's story was wonderfully sad and tragically romantic. My parents were very protective of me when it came to physical safety, but they were not at all uptight about what I heard adults say.

When Ed talked about getting drunk when his girlfriend broke up with him, my parents didn't give him a dirty look or usher me out of the room. And that was just one of many adult conversations I was a part of.

I look back and appreciate my parents trusting me and not sheltering me. While Ed was gone to basic training, I listened to a lot of his music but that album the most. I still remember that two of the songs on the album were *What's New* and *Am I Blue*, two of the great torch songs of all times. The tender and haunting lyrics touched my heart, as least as much as they could touch an adolescent girl whose dreams had not yet been shattered. I listened and I dreamed of lost love.

I hadn't had my heart broken back then, and I certainly wasn't drunk, but I listened to those songs over and over, just as Ed had. For me, it was the beginning of a life-long love affair with torch songs — those beautiful, sad songs about lost love and broken dreams that Frank Sinatra specialized in. A lot of those songs are associated with drowning your sorrows, so people who know me to be not much of a drinker are surprised that I love those sad drinking songs so much. All I can say is, "Blame it on my big brother Ed."

The Following Program is Transcribed

"Good morning. This is radio station WONA in Winona, Mississippi with studios in the Telephone Building. WONA operates on an assigned frequency of 1570 kilocycles with an operating power of one thousand watts as authorized by the Federal Communications Commission, Washington D.C. WONA is owned and operated by Southern Electronics Company, *Bob McRaney and Bob Evans partners. We invite you to stay*

tuned to WONA all day long for music, the latest world and local news, programs from the Mutual Broadcasting System, sports, and special events."

This was what Winona residents heard on their radios the morning of October 25th, 1958, when WONA signed on the air for its inaugural broadcast and again every day after that. Starting every morning at its mandated sign-on time, the station filled the broadcast day with music, news and entertainment.

The early part of the morning featured upbeat big band music and lively songs from a variety of popular singers to help people wake up and start their day on an energetic note. This was followed by a 15-minute recorded program furnished by the Navy (hosted by Pat Boone) or the Air Force (featuring the Singing Sergeants). Announcers of this era (including Bryan) were the last generation required to introduce recorded programs like these with the official sounding, "The following program is transcribed."

At 7 o'clock, it was time for the most listened to segment of the broadcast day. The Morning Edition of the News was a 15-minute recap of the latest national, state and local stories from the day and night before. Bob Chisholm wore a lot of hats. He was a radio station manager, an advertisement salesman, a PR executive, an announcer, an HR director and a programmer.

First and foremost, however, Bob Chisholm was a dedicated newsman and journalist. He would arrive at the station around 4 o'clock every morning and begin sifting through the overnight United Press International wire service stories and his own local notes before checking in on the phone with the sheriff's office. Then, fueled by black coffee and cigarettes, he started building his newscast, often working up until the last minute before airtime.

The opening was read live by the announcers who were on duty. Bob had instructed them to begin reading the introduction at 7 a.m., even if he wasn't in the studio. Quite often listeners would hear two distinct door slams in the background as Bob bolted through the control room and into the studio during the opening. Precisely on time, he would sit in front of the microphone and calmly begin, "Good morning. This is Bob Chisholm with the Morning Edition of the News."

The Morning Edition was much more than most small-town radio stations presented to their listeners. Bob spent hours crafting and recrafting a meaningful summary of world, national and local news, with emphasis on local. Unless news from other parts of the country or the world were more urgent, local events dominated the newscast. Club meetings, local sports, special events and funeral notices were woven among outside stories that had less significance to this little town. Bob's gentle, but commanding voice filled the airways with gifted phrasing, giving gravitas, authority and even levity to the stories he had so painstakingly researched, crafted and pulled together.

Once a month, Bob expanded his coverage of the morning news as he added a complete segment dedicated to a report on the monthly meeting of the Mayor and Board of Aldermen. The report was complete. It was in-depth. It was informative. Sometimes it was controversial. And sometimes the mayor and the board didn't like what they heard. In small towns (and in big towns) city leaders didn't always want voters to know everything that was talked about or voted on in public meetings. That's why politicians don't always like public meetings.

Bob was one of the reasons for this reticence. He didn't just report facts or rehash press releases. He studied and probed them and then formed his own well-developed opinion that he dutifully reported to his audience. That was just one of the reasons WONA won the Mississippi Broadcasters Association 1964 News Award for its coverage of the Mayor and Board of Aldermen.

The award came at a price. Bob endured the insults and the complaints of officials he had exposed. He sidestepped threats. He was even beaten once for his truthful reporting. Ironically, no court convictions came out of the beating, but Bob was not surprised that police corruption had won out again. He never regretted reporting the news truthfully, regardless of repercussions aimed at him.

Unless the news ran long, and it often did, it was followed by the first sponsored music program of the day, Coke Time. This was a short filler that ran until 7:45 when Leroy Anderson's "The Syncopated Clock" introduced Music, Time and Weather. *"The music is recorded, the time is Central Standard, and the Weather is official."* Today, local television stations spend two hours doing the same things WONA covered in 30 minutes to help get people ready for their day and to work and school on time.

After finishing the news, Bob would walk a couple of blocks to the post office, where he hoped to find that morning's tape of "The 20th Century Reformation Hour," (actually 30 minutes), one of the many conservative religious programs that bought time on local stations across the country.

The format for these programs was always the same. The preacher did an opening prayer for the country and then spent most of his allotted time complaining about how the government was trying to shut him down and saying he needed money from listeners to stay on the air. In fairness, he did sometimes invoke the Deity.

"My friends, I know God wants you to support my ministry. Just reach into your pockets and glorify Him with your gift."

Sometimes Bob had to wait a few minutes for the tape at the post office and would literally be threading the program onto the tape recorder as the announcer was reading the live opening.

We now present the 20th Century Reformation Hour featuring Dr. Carl McIntire,. pastor of the Bible Presbyterian Church in Collingswood, New Jersey. And now, here is Dr. McIntire with his cheery greeting.

Bob or the announcer would hit play and Dr. McIntire would burst forth with, "Good morning, Good morning," followed by his anti-communist or anti big government slogan of the day. "We all know Khrushchev is a man of peace. A piece here, a piece there, until he has it all." A popular element of the broadcast was Dr. McIntire's sycophant sidekick, associate pastor "Amen Charlie" whose only function seemed to be shouting, "Amen" at appropriate (or inappropriate) intervals. He was very good at it. After listeners had gotten their fill of Dr. McIntire, or 30 minutes later – whichever came last – it was time for more music, interrupted only by a short recap of the news at 10 o'clock. More music filled the rest of the morning.

The Noon Edition of the News signaled the mid-point of the broadcast day. Bob was always out gathering news for the next morning's Morning Edition, selling ads or trying to take a short nap in his cubicle that served as a barely private office, so it fell to the announcer on duty to gather stories from the UPI teletype, put them in some usable order and hopefully read them at least once before going on the air. This was a naïve, very optimistic and seldom achieved goal.

Part of the 15-minute noon newscast was the daily farm report. As Bryan remembers it, he usually had had no idea what he was reading. He was a city boy, not a farmer. Fortunately, he was dating the daughter of the Assistant County Agent, so he called the agent and asked, "What the heck am I reading?" Mr. Wilson patiently explained hog, beef, grain, bean and cotton futures so Bryan could at least sound as if he knew what he was talking about. The conversation was enlightening.

If you ever want to know what "fair to middlin" cotton grade means, just ask Bryan. He still remembers and is eager to share the information. That arrangement worked fine for a while, until the day Bryan didn't take the time to read his stories ahead of time. He was halfway into the second story when he realized he was giving a very detailed explanation of how to castrate a pig. Somehow, he extricated himself. It wasn't pretty, it wasn't clever and it didn't work. Bob, of course, heard the broadcast and gently suggested that perhaps reading stories ahead of time might prevent this sort of thing from happening again. Bryan thought this was good advice, especially since his girlfriend mentioned how funny her father thought the incident was.

One of the locally favorite shows came next. Swap Shop, in its various versions, was a staple of local programming across the country – but not always done like it was in the South. The station invited listeners to call in live or write the station with items they wanted to swap, buy or sell.

There seemed to be no limit to the number or kinds of items people were interested in getting rid of or buying. The quarter hour was filled with phone calls interspersed with two announcers taking turns reading items from a box of index cards that was updated every day by the secretary who took calls and didn't ask questions. With all the changes, it was often impossible to check the cards ahead of time.

Instead, DJs had to read them "cold" with no preparation. That's how Bryan got caught one day reading a card that said (sic), "For sale, one <u>heffer</u> bull." He stumbled through a correction and then moved on to the next item. After the program, he asked the secretary if she knew the difference between a Hereford and a heifer. She didn't.

For those who didn't grow up near a farm or date the daughter of the Assistant County Agent, a heifer is a female cow of any breed. A Hereford is a specific breed of cow. A Hereford can be a heifer or a bull, but it can't be both. Part of the fun of doing the show was getting to the cards a few minutes ahead of time and making sure the other guy got the weird items to read. That was the extent of the preparation.

The program was fun because of the variety of things people wanted to buy, sell, or swap. Offerings ran from homemade jelly to adult potty chairs, to "Three dozen hens and enough roosters to take care of the whole flock." What made it more interesting was that all the phone calls were live with no sissy seven second delays like you find on talk shows today. What the caller said was exactly what the audience heard, even the man who said he was, "…getting rid of my chickens because I have too damn many of them to deal with." It was like being helmsman of the Titanic and pushing the throttle forward while the iceberg warnings were coming in during the night. While nobody ever hit the iceberg, many new (and a few experienced) announcers did manage to scrape a few along the way. It was live local radio at its best.

As a side note, calling the station was easy. It was like living in Mayberry. Listeners just picked up the phone and told the operator, "Give me 1570" or, "Ring the radio station for me." The phone number was the same as the frequency of the station on the AM dial and was easy to remember. WONA studios were on the second floor of the Telephone Building where the operators answered, plugged and re-plugged calls all day and all night right next to the station. Maurice Gooch, Chief Engineer and announcer, was dating and later married one of the operators.

Sometimes Peggy would call and ask him to get food for her and the other operators. No problem, except the door to the phone room was locked and they weren't allowed to let anyone in who was not a phone company employee.

Maurice had to stand on the street and throw bags of sandwiches up to the second-floor window as he delivered lunch. Dating an operator did offer one problem for Gooch. Young girls would sometimes call the studio and flirt with the announcers. Peggy knew Maurice's schedule and more than once told a caller, "Honey, you're not talking to him. He's mine." and refused to put the call through.

There were no conservative talk radio stations in the late fifties and early sixties. There were, however, ultra-conservative radio programs that bought time on local stations to air their views. These paid programs were a good source of income for stations and aired around the country. Oil Billionaire H.L. Hunt (his son, Lamar, was one of the founders of the American Football League) aired his radical viewpoints each weekday in a 15-minute program that ran during the noon hour each day. "Lifeline" was written and hosted by Melvin Munn and sponsored by a Hunt subsidiary, HLH foods. The program took on communism, the government and a variety of moral issues, all delivered with a tone that seemed to suggest tomorrow was just about to be cancelled.

"Lifeline" aired on over 500 small stations across the country, each one receiving a weekly shipment of five programs to air. Gaps were left in the tape so local announcers could read live commercials. While they were reading, the DJs had to keep one eye on the VU (volume unit) meter to see when the next segment started. Still reading the live commercial, the announcer had to hit "stop" and then back up the tape manually until the meter quit moving. At the end of the commercial, another audible click indicated the tape was rolling again for another program segment.

The one o'clock hour brought a perspective seldom seen in radio stations in the sixties. "Mainly for Women" looked at life and entertainment from a woman's point of view. The program was researched, written and hosted by Bob's wife Carol, a radio pioneer in her own right.

Carol scoured wire services, newspapers and magazines for features that would interest women. She had a discerning eye for what would appeal to this often-neglected audience. Her smooth, soothing voice added another dimension to the program as she taped it from home every weekday and either sent it to the station by special courier (Bob returning from lunch) or brought it to the station herself. Her meticulous notes told the announcers where to insert commercials and even detailed what songs should be played. It was an entertaining show that helped define women's programming for the time. "Mainly for Women" had a loyal audience of women and men and won several awards from the Mississippi Broadcasters Association. There were no specific categories for women's programs. Carol won against male competition, a formidable achievement in those days.

Then it was back to the music as WONA Bandstand highlighted a different artist or big band each 15 minutes for the next hour. That sounds easy enough – until a DJ would sometimes try to get too clever. That's when something sometimes falls under the category, "Gee, at the time it seemed like a good idea." It usually wasn't.

A lovely old lady from New York City had made a name for herself by regularly sitting on the front row of the Ed Sullivan Show as well as many of the game shows that taped in the city. Mrs. Miller became a cult favorite with fans and TV hosts alike. She also loved to sing. She also couldn't sing. She was so bad that her cult following loved to listen to her and often encouraged the host to let her sing (assault is a better word) a tune. She even recorded an album, a screeching, caterwauling compilation of almost unrecognizable standards and current hits. WONA was sent a promotional copy which all the announcers wisely ignored, except for the new kid who thought it would be a great idea to feature Mrs. Miller on a 15-minute segment of Bandstand.

Bryan quickly realized if a little of something good goes a long way, a minutia of something bad goes on a long and torturous journey through the nine circles of hell. Mrs. Miller was not even halfway through "These Boots Were Made for Walking" when Bob walked into the control room, looked at Bryan, grimaced, and walked out shaking his head. Bryan got the message. As the song faded – none too soon – he opened the mic and said, "I don't know about you, but I think that's enough for Mrs. Miller today. Why don't we just go into our next featured artist, Perry Como." Bryan put the record back into the album sleeve and meekly walked into Bob's office. Bob took the Mrs. Miller album from Bryan's sheepishly outstretched hand and tossed it into the trash. He never said a word. His look was enough.

Bandstand was followed at 3 o'clock by the fourth newscast of the day. This 15-minute roundup concentrated on national and state stories of the day and was supplemented with features or special local stories taken from the Morning Edition of the News. Sometimes an extra announcer would be available and would deliver the news from the small studio next to the control room. Since there was no control panel (board) in the studio, the on-duty announcer would introduce the news and then turn on the desk-top studio microphone.

One afternoon, having nothing better to do, Bryan realized Ed Forsythe, a very capable and much more experienced announcer, was somewhat helpless as he read the news live with no control over his microphone. Bryan walked into the studio and picked up the mic, forcing Ed to stand up in order to be heard properly.

One of them found this to be quite amusing so Bryan started walking around the studio, carrying the microphone at the end of the very long cable. Since he had no other alternative, Ed was forced to follow Bryan as he continued to read the news.

Round and round they went, covering every nook and cranny of the studio, sometimes walking slowly and sometimes walking faster as Bryan moved the mic up and down and from side to side. Ed followed obligingly, if reluctantly. Then Bryan delivered the coup de grâce. He got down on all fours and crawled under the open bottomed studio table, holding the mic almost at floor level and forcing Ed to prop himself on his elbows as he continued to read.

Just as Ed got comfortable, Bryan started moving again. Now he was leading a visibly unhappy announcer who was completely under his control – until a menacing smile spread across Ed's face as he finished a story.

"We'll be right back," he told the unknowing audience, "Right after this message from our sponsor."

There was only one problem. The on-duty announcer had to read the live commercial, which was sitting above the console in the now unoccupied control room. At that moment, however, he was crawling under the table in the studio with a microphone in his hands and looking at the now grinning newsman he had been leading around like a stray puppy.

Bryan set the microphone down as gently and quickly as he could, rose to his feet, and scurried into the control room. As he threw the switch, the on-air light in the studio dimmed and Ed burst out laughing, forcing Bryan to close the door before reading the commercial. He scrambled for the commercial, took a quick breath, and tried to sound calm as he read the message. When the newscast was over, Ed walked in the control room, smirked and said, "You're good kid, but as long as I'm around you're second best."

Once the news was over, it was time for more music – but not before a five-minute update of all the news from Winona High School delivered by a 15-year-old student, somewhere in the never-never land between verbal acne and shaving. Bryan diligently reported everything of interest going on at school, except for that time his senior year when he was expelled for trying to start a riot and take over the school.

The 1570 Club followed, the station's only step into the overheated waters of Rock and Roll, where Elvis, Simon and Garfunkel, Herman's Hermits, the Righteous Brothers, the Rolling Stones and the Beatles pushed aside Frankie Lane, Vaughn Monroe, Tony Bennett, Tennessee Ernie Ford, Perry Como, The Four Aces, and the Maguire Sisters. This was two hours of music dedicated to young baby-boomers. WONA was a small station and was generally not on the list of stations that got free promotional records.

Despite his feelings to the contrary, Bryan soon realized he wasn't an influential DJ on the caliber of WLS's Dick Bionde or WHBQ's Jack Parnell (who later became a close friend). He somehow talked (begged?) Bob into giving him $15 to go down to

Tardy Furniture to replenish the station's somewhat meager library of current rock music.

Armed with that 1963 small fortune, Bryan went around the corner to the store, the only place in town young people could buy their kind of music. For just 99 cents anyone could buy a hit record after listening to it on the old 45 rpm player in the upstairs storage area of the store. Because the owner's son Tommy was Bryan's friend, and because Tardy Furniture was a regular sponsor on the station, the $15 investment allowed Bryan to walk away with a bonanza of 25 records for the now overflowing library of Rock and Roll hits. Bob must have had a special reverence for the music played on the 1570 Club. He put the 45 rpm records in their own special box to keep them safe. He labeled the box, "Rock and Roll. Do Not Mix With Real Music."

In the ensuing years, Bryan was lucky enough to work with many of the people whose records he had played, before and after the Rock and Roll explosion. Some even became friends. Two of his more memorable encounters had direct connections to the music he had played on the radio as a teenager.

Nashville pianist Floyd Cramer was a guest on a television special Bryan was producing in 1986. His hit, "Last Date" had reached #2 on the charts (although it was #1 on the list of songs for slow dancing). The flip side or "B" side was a little-known up-tempo song called, "Flip, Flop and Bop" and was used as the theme song for the 1570 Club.

Years later when Floyd asked Bryan what song he wanted him to play he immediately answered, "Flip, Flop and Bop." Floyd stared at Bryan and said, "Where the hell did you hear that song?"

When he explained the song's personal significance, Cramer smiled and said, "You got it." He even dedicated the song to him as the momentary personal concert went over the air to millions of people.

Ten years later Bryan was discussing song selection with guest star Bobby Vinton, the "Polish Prince," whose "Roses are Red" hit was a favorite during the high school years of the sixties. Bryan told Bobby he had a special feeling for that song because an old girlfriend had once asked him to sing that song to her. You guessed it. Another personal concert. Suzainne, wherever you are, Bryan hopes you saw the show. The song was for you. Incidentally, she never asked Bryan to sing to her again.

The two-hour blast of youthful exuberance gave way to the more sedate end of the broadcast day. Twilight Time, "Music that's easy to listen to, easy on the nerves. The perfect ending to a perfect day." Especially if you have already been on the air for 12 hours as often was the case during the Bob and Bryan marathons in the late 60s. The music was quiet, soothing, peacef…zzzzzzzz. More than once, Bryan woke up to the most frightening sound a young DJ can hear, the hissing of a record "tracking" as it spun around and around, long past the end of the album that had just played front to back as he peacefully napped.

Even more frightening was the sound of the control room telephone ringing and jolting him awake. Bryan would grab the phone, blurt, "I got it!" and then hang up. He didn't have to ask who it was. Bob never chastised him for falling asleep.

With the hours Bob kept, the same thing had happened more than once to him as well. As Twilight time eased to a close and the sun was poised to set, the broadcast ended with an FCC mandated sign-off and an invitation for listeners to tune in the next morning.

With a majestic, "Ladies and Gentlemen, our national anthem,"

The Star Spangled Banner brought an official end to the broadcast day.

Mixed in with all the "glamour and fame" of being a small-town radio announcer, there was also a lot of work. Before each shift, and certainly well before program consultants and automation, the announcers' first job was to select music for his shift. In the 50s and 60s, almost all announcers were men. Carol Chisholm was a rare and welcome exception.

Music selection wasn't as easy as it might seem. The DJ couldn't just select the songs he liked. He had to understand the listening habits of the audience. He had to make sure he didn't play too many female artists in a row (popular male singers outnumbered their female counterparts more than 2-1). Instrumentals had to be carefully placed and tempos had to be varied. It was also important to give special attention not only to the national popularity of artists and songs, but also to local tastes.

On top of all this, the DJ had to make sure the record he selected had already not been played by someone else a little earlier – or that he had not played the same song at the same time the day before. Since almost all of the songs were on albums, it was important to be able to remember what song was on what album. Most DJs liked to "pull" (select) all their music just before their shift started. The albums would be put in order and stacked on an open counter space right next to the console.

At WONA, the albums were filed in alphabetical order, according to artist, in a big shelf right behind the announcer. In theory, after a song was played, the DJ would put the vinyl back in the cover and immediately refile it. At least, that was the theory. In reality, DJs hated filing albums and usually left them in a pile to be dealt with at the end of the shift, unless they were able to find an eager, gullible 12-year-old who saw refiling albums as his gateway to the glamour of one day being on the air.

Long after sign-off, there was plenty to do. In addition to catching up on all the paperwork that had been neglected during the broadcast day, announcers often spent an hour or more writing and recording new commercials and catching up on neglected or postponed broadcast logs and FCC reports.

How, you may ask, could an announcer with all those tasks and responsibilities possibly have time to take care of urgent "personal matters" that might arise during his shift, especially at a time when almost every record ran less than two minutes?

Fortunately, country singer Marty Robbins, the patron saint of all disc jockeys, unknowingly provided a solution in September 1958 when he released a four minute and thirty-eight second epic about a man willing to die for the attention of the fair maiden, Falina. *El Paso* shot to the top of the charts and became the number one (and number two) favorite song of every DJ in America. The song served other purposes as well.

In late 1966, Bob and Bryan were the only two people at the station for a couple of months. On days Bob was not able to relieve him for lunch, Bryan would call McDougal's Drugstore and order a hamburger and fries from their soda fountain. As soon as he started playing *El Paso*, Bryan would scurry out of the control room, run down the stairs, dash up the street, and hurry into the drugstore. After hastily exchanging a dollar bill for the sack containing his lunch and change, he would backtrack his route, burst into the control room, and seat himself just before the song started to fade.

After a deep breath, he would open the mic and calmly introduce the next song. If he was lucky, he might also have had time for a quick bathroom stop. Bryan claims that, to this day, when he hears that song, he has the sudden urge to…well, never mind.

The Four Seasons (Plus Christmas)

There were four seasons in the Old South: Football Season, Hunting Season, Fishing Season and Election Season. Bob loved Election Season. From a pure business perspective, politicians spend a lot of money to buy advertising. From the viewpoint of a journalist, elections meant keeping up and even fact-checking who was saying what about whom. Bob loved writing about campaigns and campaigners. It was important to him to present a balanced and unbiased view of the elections and the candidates. As always, Bob threw himself enthusiastically into the challenge.

As the county seat of Montgomery County, Winona was in the center of the political arena. Statewide candidates mingled with county and local hopefuls and fought for the attention of the voters. Flatbed trailers repurposed as stages were hauled in by tractors and parked in front of the courthouse so these politicians could gather and try to mesmerize and seduce their constituents. And the crowds came. They came to hear the Southern gospel quartets and the wannabe country bands that drew the masses to the stage. Warming up the crowd was easy in the dusty, sweltering heat of the August primaries. Young boys moved among the crowds, handing out cooling fans imprinted with the names of local funeral homes or hawking cold cokes for 10 cents each as they pocketed a hefty 100 percent profit. In the south, any soft drink was a coke. "What kind of coke do you want? Co-cola, RC, Orange Crush, Pepsi, Grapette?" This custom always bothered Bryan's good friend Paula Hood, whose father co- owned the local Pepsi Bottling Company that also produced Dr. Pepper, Orange Crush and Grapette.

Once the crowd was gathered and entertained, it was time for the office seekers to take the stage, ties loosened and suit coats draped over their arms and usually clutching a colorful bandana to wipe away the sweat that poured from their faces. One by one, each man (they were almost always men at that time) took charge of the platform and the crowd for his allotted time — shouting, whispering, strutting, dancing and imploring the audience with the zeal of an old Southern preacher. It was the best entertainment you could find for the price. Ironically, and despite the plagiarism of that distinctive gospel style, political speeches in the '50s and '60s South were only meant for white audiences.

Voter registration and participation in the Black community were just beginning to make their way southward. Because of lingering, vivid remembrances of Republican Reconstruction after the Civil War, almost all the viable candidates were Democrats. Elections were settled in the Democratic primary, never in the general election. Candidates railed against each other, fought, scrapped, and accused opponents of every malicious misdeed and incompetency possible. That is, until the primary was decided.

At that moment, the party unanimously united behind the triumphant candidate who suddenly became a shining example of morality, leadership and political integrity. It was an amazing transformation. From this dichotomy, the term "Yellow Dog Democrat" emerged. If a well-qualified Republican competed against a mangy yellow dog running as a Democrat, it was said, the yellow dog would win.

Bryan loved election week and election day. Because WONA was only allowed by the FCC to broadcast in the daytime, over-the air election coverage abilities were limited in the evening. Bob, of course, had another novel solution that benefited the listeners, without violating the strict rules of the FCC. He simply built on the model of the station's night-time college football coverage and expanded it to provide up-to-the-minute election coverage after WONA went off the air for the evening.

During the week before the election, Bryan set up speakers and chairs in the Winona Community House and in nearby Kilmichael for closed-circuit coverage of the evening vote count. Bob paid Bryan $15 to do this, a reminder of the wealth that awaited Bryan on the radio. That was more than three times what Bryan made for 14½ hours of bagging chickens and grinding hamburger meat at Piggly Wiggly on Saturdays.

On election morning, Bryan, when he was young, and his younger brothers Joe and Jimmy got up early for their regular election day enterprise. Candidates looking for last minute votes would pay them a princely $5 each to stand near the entrance to the polls and pass out their leftover campaign business cards to everyone as they came to cast their ballots. The boys always solicited candidates from different political races to increase their earnings. On a good election day, they would each get as many as five candidates, making sure voters got one card from each potential public servant.

Of course, they never handed out cards for two candidates running for the same office. That was left to fellow entrepreneurs. It was fun to watch the adults wind their way through the gauntlet of business cards and flyers in order to vote. W.W. Jenkins, the gregarious one-armed owner of the City Café, always came prepared for the onslaught of campaign literature. He strode through the melee with a cigar box in his hand, offering it so cards could be deposited (sometimes tossed). Then, without breaking stride, he ceremoniously dumped all the cards into the big trash can just outside election headquarters as he went in to cast his ballot.

As soon as the polls closed, Bryan would run inside for his second duty of the day, assisting in coverage of the vote count. For the rest of the night, he ran back and forth between the Community House and the nearby courthouse as Bob, usually assisted by accountant Billy Flowers, compiled the tallied votes and reported results to the assembled crowds.

As information came in from the designated reporter in Kilmichael, Bob would share that as well. This is just another example of why WONA and other-small town stations became such an integral part of the community. The whole crew stayed with their coverage until all the results were known. That was back when elections were fun.

The vote count itself was a fascinating process. Long before computers and calculators, all voting and vote counting was done by hand. People stood in line to have their registration checked, received a paper ballot and pencil and went inside the booth to make their choices. The ballot was then folded and dropped through a slot into an actual locked ballot box. As soon as the polls closed, the boxes were assembled and, in front of a large crowd of candidates, families and interested spectators, they were then unlocked and opened so the votes could be counted. The process was completely open, and as they say today, transparent.

A designated clerk would unlock each box, reach into it, bring out a single ballot, and pass it to a reader who would loudly call out the vote for each office. As each name was called, a tabulator would announce the count as "1, 2, 3, 4, or Tally", indicating every fifth vote by drawing a diagonal line through the four previous marks.

The same ballot would then be passed to a second reader who would again state the names as a second tabulator announced the count. Once an official ruled the two counts were identical, the ballot was handed to the threader, who put a large needle through the middle of the ballot and pulled it along a piece of yarn until the ballot rested on top of the previous one.

This continued until the string of yarn was full. The ballots were then tied off and put aside in plain sight, indicating they had been counted. When the ballot box was empty, the clerk picked it up, turned it upside down, showed the empty container to the crowd, and unlocked the next box. At the end of the evening, two sets of tabulators independently tallied their vote totals and, if they matched, a winner was declared.

The process was a long, tedious, and fascinating way to spend an election night. No predictions. No exit polls. No endless commentary. Just votes, tabulations and results. Maybe that's how elections should be done today. Possibly that system would make it harder for any candidate and his or her supporters to accuse election officials of fraud.

Elections were only held once every two to four years, but Christmas, of course, was an annual event. The holidays were special and lasted several weeks. Downtown merchants decorated their stores and the city put wreaths, garlands and lights on anything that didn't move. The annual Christmas parade featured the Winona High School band, surrounded by floats, cars full of beauty queens and city officials, Santa Claus, and horses and riders from the Confederate Cavalry. Marching right behind the mounted Confederate Cavalry while wearing white shoes was always an adventure for the band, especially for the young DJ who was carrying the big bass drum and couldn't see where he was stepping.

The sidewalks were filled, and people spilled out onto the streets as they gathered early to get a good look at the parade. Half the town was marching in the parade and the other half was watching. Teenaged carolers from all the churches wandered the neighborhoods with their festive holiday sounds, pausing sometimes to enjoy the hot chocolate and Christmas cookies served by their appreciative family audiences.

WONA was always right in the middle of these celebrations. Christmas music filled the air all day long, both over-the-air and through the speakers outside the second story studios. The radio station didn't just play Christmas songs. It brought the entire community into the celebration. Bob, Maurice Gooch, Bryan and other announcers would take microphones, recorders and mobile control boards around town to record Christmas cantatas from various churches and special concerts from groups like the J.J. Knox High School Choir. WONA aired all of them and everyone listened.

No one worked harder before and during the Christmas holidays than Bob. In addition to managing the station, selling advertising and gathering and reporting news, Bob personally programmed the Christmas music lineup for its entire run every year. He wanted to make sure listeners were treated to just the right blend of music, guaranteeing the same songs weren't played too close together or at the same time every day.

Bob cleverly mixed instrumentals, artists, big bands, male and female singers, novelty songs and local groups and churches. He labored countless hours to make sure everything was just right. The work was tedious, but it paid off. Bob Chisholm made the effort, but the listeners got the benefit. And Bryan and Candy got to learn first-hand the importance of detail and hard work.

Hometown Sports

Sports coverage, both local high school and statewide college, was a rallying point for the community. Friday night football was a mandatory destination for adults and students alike in Winona. If going to the game was a ritual, WONA's Saturday morning playback of the previous night's game was a required start to the weekend. Fans who had attended the game just a few hours earlier gathered around their radios to listen, either to relive, or to bemoan what they had experienced the night before.

Winona mayor and TV repair shop owner Fred Watts was the unanimous choice to be both the play-by-play commentator and the stadium's PA announcer. Fred had one unmatched qualification. He owned all the equipment. Armed with his microphone, speakers, cables and trusty Norelco reel-to-reel tape recorder, the Voice of the Tigers diligently prepared for his weekly Friday night ritual.

Sometimes on game day, he even climbed into the speaker truck politicians would hire so they could do mobile campaigning. Instead of making announcements for politicians or reminding people about grocery specials at Piggly Wiggly or Middleton's Grocery, he cruised a busy downtown Winona urging people to come to that night's game against Indianola, Grenada, South Panola or whoever the latest Delta Valley Conference opponent was.

With Fred, you got the whole package: equipment, stadium announcer, radio play-by-play commentator and promotions manager. It wasn't for the money. His daughter Carole Watts Graves recalls that school Superintendent M.P. Smith made Fred pay his way into the games he was furnishing equipment for and also announcing for free. But Fred was dedicated. He even drove to out-of-town games at his own expense to record the games for the Saturday morning playbacks.

Fred had a system for mixing his game public address duties with his play-by-play responsibilities. He would first announce the results to the fans in the stadium and then he would turn on the recorder to reconstruct the play for Saturday's radio audience. The system worked well. Most of the time. Sometimes, in the heat of the game, Fred would mix up his dual responsibilities.

Carole's husband, Bob Graves, who played guard for the Tigers, recalls one night when WHS was locked in a tight battle with nearby rival Grenada:

"It was fourth down and Grenada was getting ready to punt. Fred's PA area was right next to the Grenada coaches' booth, and he overheard them call for a fake punt.

All of a sudden, the crowd and the players on the field heard, "Well, it looks like the Bulldogs are lining up to try a fake punt. Let's hope the Winona boys are ready for it."

I turned to tackle Billy Murphy and said, "Murph, did he just say what I thought he said?"

At that moment, Grenada snapped the ball and ran right past us for a touchdown."

In another game, Winona's punt returner fielded a high punt and then cut, darted and sprinted his way up the field for a spectacular touchdown. Fans in the stadium were treated to an enthusiastic and detailed description of the run, complete with "Oh boy" and "look at him go!" The next morning, fans huddled around the radio to listen to a replay of this game winning run.

As they held their collective breaths in anticipation, Fred nonchalantly announced, "And on the last play, Winona's Leon Felts ran 87 yards for a touchdown."

Let's face it, Fred Watts was no Al Michaels. Then again, Al Michaels was no Fred Watts. Winona fans would vote for Fred.

High school football wasn't the only sports passion in town. Like most other Mississippi communities, Winona was equally and passionately divided by loyalties to the Ole Miss Rebels and the Mississippi State Bulldogs. Everyone who couldn't go to the games wanted to listen to them on the radio. The only problem was that WONA was required to go off the air at sundown every day. Winter made that time even earlier. Because of this, the station was only able to broadcast daytime games that ended before sundown. That meant fans without special FM radios that could pick up distant signals couldn't hear the night games.

   Always on the lookout for a way to expand WONA's reach into the community, Bob came up with a simple, but ingenious plan. Games for both schools were broadcast on traditional AM radio. Even the stronger signals didn't have a long reach. To boost the signal, the schools also aired their games on the new FM radio technology. FM was not very popular at the time, so most people didn't buy these newer and more expensive radios. Bob did. Whenever one of the schools had a night game, WONA took the FM radio to the Community House where Bryan helped set up speakers and chairs so fans could listen to the evening games. The station even provided free sandwiches, snacks and drinks. WONA didn't make any money for this service. The station even had to pay for the refreshments and rental for the Community House. What Bob and the station did earn, though, was the undying appreciation of the town as fans were able to gather and listen to their favorite team on Saturday night, just the way God intended.

   Bryan got his first sportscasting break when he was 16 years old. Bob called him into his office and asked if he had ever done basketball play-by-play announcing. Bob knew the answer, of course. Without waiting for Bryan's reply, he said, "Do you think you could do it?" He also knew what Bryan's answer would be to that question.

Winona was playing in a tournament in nearby Eupora, and Bob was ready to try WONA's first live sportscast. Arrangements had already been made. Sponsors had already come on board. All he needed to complete the package was an experienced play-by-play announcer, or at least someone who THOUGHT he was experienced. The plan was to broadcast three or more games (girls' and boys' teams), depending on how well the teams did in the tournament. "Oh, by the way, I'll pay you $7.50 a game." What? $7.50 for each game? Bryan already knew radio was fun. This was the first time he realized he could also get rich.

On the morning of the first two games, Bryan and Chief Engineer Maurice Gooch loaded the small mobile control board, a headset, two microphones and the necessary wires into Gooch's car and set out for the 25-mile drive to Eupora. Thirty minutes after they got to the gym, the broadcast was set up and ready to go. The Winona girls were playing in the opening game. When he went on the air before that first game, Bryan described the beautiful shiny basketball court and remarked how nice it looked. As he was speaking, the two teams ran onto the floor for warm-ups…and slid halfway across the court. It was at that moment school officials learned the janitor had decided he wanted the court to look

Maurice Gooch   Photo courtesy Bryan Cottingham.

World vs. Bob Chisholm

impressive for the tournament. He had stayed up all night, on his own time and meticulously waxed the entire floor. It looked great! And there was absolutely no way people could even walk on, much less run up and down the court playing basketball.

Workers and volunteers were dispatched to bring hard-bristled brooms and wheelbarrows of sand into the gym. For the next three quarters of an hour they scoured, scraped and swept the floor, stripping all the wax and half the paint off the now defiled court. The janitor wept. Bless his well-intentioned heart.

Meanwhile, the novice announcer was suddenly faced with an unexpected 45 minutes of airtime to fill, with no preparation. It never occurred to him to just toss the broadcast back to the station to have them fill the time with music until the game started. Bryan was being paid $7.50 to talk, so he talked. And he talked. He described the scene. He interviewed fans. He talked.

He brought in his good friend Larry Wilson, captain of the boys' team that was playing next. They talked. They analyzed the chances of the girls' team and even discussed the offerings from the refreshment stands. The popcorn was too salty. Finally, the game started. Larry hung around to provide color commentary until halftime, when he had to depart to get ready for his game. The girls won the game easily, giving Bryan the chance to fall into a comfortable rhythm with his first broadcast. The drama seemed over for the afternoon. It was only beginning.

The boys' team was a 20-point underdog to a bigger and faster team from Louisville, Mississippi.. It looked as if Bryan's biggest challenge was going to be making a lopsided game seem interesting. Five minutes into the game, an excitement started to build as the underdog Tigers kept the game close with great shooting and defensive hustle, even taking the lead a couple of times. Bryan's thick Southern accent described the action ("He passes the ball to number fowty-fow. The score is tahd at thirty non to thirty non"), all the while engaging in a losing battle with a voice still held hostage by puberty. For those who don't speak fluent Southern: "He passes the ball to number 44. The score is tied at 39 to 39."

The struggle on the court continued. With only 15 seconds left in the game, Winona had a one-point lead and the ball. Louisville fouled in desperation. The pitch of the now veteran's voice increased as everyone waited for the two free throws that would guarantee this upset victory. First one shot and then the other bounced off the rim. Louisville scurried up the court with only seven seconds left in the game. Bryan's voice climbed to an almost undistinguishable crescendo as they desperately tried to find an open shot. Then, only moments before the clock ran down, a Louisville player flung a desperate 20 foot shot blindly at the basket.

The crowd held its breath. Bryan waited. The teams waited. The listeners at home waited. "Nooooooooo," Bryan screamed, oblivious of the fact he was on the radio. "LOUISVILLE SHOOTS AND WINS!" Bryan still has a recording of that game. Sixty years later, it brings back some really embarrassing memories that elicit a lot of laughs from his kids and grandkids.

There is an epilogue to the story. Because the first game had started so late, the conclusion of this game was pushing the very strict sign-off time mandated by the FCC. Facing a potential fine, the studio announcer back in Winona stayed with the game as long as he dared, even rushing through a highly truncated version of the sign-off. With 30 seconds left in the game, and Winona improbably in the lead, WONA fell silent.

The station didn't subscribe to a ratings service, but if the phone calls that assaulted the station to find out the final score were any indication, everyone in Winona was listening.

Local Pickers and That Old Time Religion

Small town radio stations didn't just play records from national artists. Local music was not ignored. Almost 50 years ago, the Statler Brothers released a still popular album featuring mythical country singer Lester "Roadhog" Moran and his Cadillac Cowboys. The satirical album was based on the very real experiences of small radio stations across the South who all seemed to air a live Saturday morning program featuring a local country band.

WONA was no exception. Every week, local photographer Clayton Tyler lugged his guitar and his small band up the stairs and into the studios to play down-home country songs for his fans. There was something to be said about Clayton's music. Bless his heart, he was a good photographer. In the South, you could say anything bad about a person with impunity, as long as you preceded the comment with "Bless his heart."

For 15 minutes each Saturday morning, his familiar upbeat tunes shared the airways with lonesome renditions of faded love, heartache, lost dogs and shattered dreams. Almost every Saturday, Clayton and the band closed their moment in the spotlight the same way. "Folks," he would drawl with a tear in his voice, "We don't usually repeat songs, but this week we got a couple of letters asking us to bring back an old favorite of ours and, I hope, yours. For those folks who wrote in, here is our version of the classic, "Long Black Veil." Let 'er go, boys."

At best, "Long Black Veil" is a truly sad song about a man who is sent to the gallows for a murder he didn't commit, refusing to tell the jury he was innocent because he was "in the arms of my best friend's wife" at the time of the killing. Looking back, he probably should have re-evaluated his choice, because his scarlet lady stood quietly by as he was hanged. His only consolation was that she often walked the hills of the cemetery late at night, wearing a long black veil as she lamented his death.

Clayton and his band pulled every possible emotion from the song as they strummed and sang and strummed and sang…and strummed and sang. It seemed as if Clayton would never get to his signature farewell, "Thanks for tuning in, folks. Good Lord willin' we'll be back again next week at this same time. So long, everybody."

If Saturday mornings were for local bands and football replays, Sundays belonged to the preachers. Local churches, almost always Baptist, brought the gospel in words and music to the masses. Bryan was in the control room one Sunday morning, grabbing a much-needed nap, when he was suddenly awakened by an enthusiastic "Hallelujah" as the preacher slammed his open hand on the table. He almost fell out of his chair. Another preacher always brought his bulky tape recorder and would intersperse his morning sermon with, "a number from our choir" as he paused, leaned over and loudly clicked the Play button to bring them in, and then pushed the equally noisy Stop button as they finished their song.

For as long as anyone in Winona can remember, the 11 o'clock hour on Sunday was filled by the First Baptist Church, the biggest congregation in town. All across the South, weekly radio services like this brought joy and comfort to the people who couldn't make it to church that day. In many cases, the Sunday morning services were the only real contact people were able to have with their church families. Radio was their lifeline.

Every Sunday morning, Bob hauled the remote equipment down the street to the First Baptist Church, set it up, turned it on and pulled out his transistor radio to make sure the signal was being broadcast. After the service or sometimes on Monday morning, he would return to the church to unhook and retrieve the mobile unit and take it back to the station.

Anyone who sees this as a mocking look at life in the small towns of the South needs to think again. To be honest, people liked all of this. It didn't matter if it was polished or sophisticated. Listeners didn't care that it wasn't Broadway or that it wasn't always good. They cared and they listened because it was local. It came from friends and neighbors and that made it better than Broadway. But please don't play "Long Black Veil" when Bryan is around. Bryan found out many years later that his wife's uncle wrote that song. Bryan has always regretted that he never got the chance to strangle him.

Winona streets in the 1950s and early 1960s, when sidewalks were filled with people (above) and today when the sidewalks are not so busy. Photos courtesy Bryan Cottingham.

Chapter 3

The Killer Sheriff

On January 3, 1960, Bob, who was 30 at the time, covered the first really big story of his career — a story so shocking and sensational that it was reported in national news.

In the early morning hours of that Sunday, Deputy Sheriff William Lee Kelly, a 27-year-old, who was described in the Winona Times as having "a winsome smile and a friendly disposition," was found in the sheriff's office vault of the Montgomery County Courthouse. He had been stabbed, slashed and bludgeoned to death with a ball-peen hammer.

It would soon come out that Deputy Kelly was working late on Saturday night at his desk when two men — Alec Morris, 50, and Pink Earl Townsend, 26, using a key given to them by Sheriff Lawrence King, burst through the office door and held a gun on Kelly, forcing him to crawl into the nearby vault, where the young deputy was murdered.

The next morning Bob was allowed into the crime scene with the Winona police, one of whom seemed to be taking constant notes, but when Bob looked over the officer's shoulder, he was stunned to realize the policeman must have been illiterate because his notes were nothing but nonsense scribbling with no words on the page. Even though Bob did not include that fact in his news coverage of the murder, it was the beginning of a 10-year rocky relationship between Chisholm and the Winona police.

On the night of the murder, Morris and Townsend, who had

gotten a $300 advance, left the courthouse and drove down Highway 51 to pick up the rest of their $1,000 murder-for-hire fee. Two days later, Morris and Townsend were charged with murder after Townsend confessed to his part in the crime. Lawrence King, who was just days from finishing his term as sheriff, was charged with murder on January 6.

King, whose defense attorney was former Mississippi Governor J. P. Coleman, was granted a change of venue, and the trial was held in Meridian, Mississippi. Bob drove to Meridian every day of the trial and drove back to Winona each night (two hours each way) so he could report on the trial during his morning newscast the next day.

The state's two main witnesses were Alec Morris, who had pleaded guilty to carrying out the murder, and Mrs. Minnie Kelly, the deputy's young widow. Mrs. Kelly, whom a Jackson newspaper described as "a pretty 23-year-old brunette," testified that 51-year-old Sheriff King had tried to have sexual relations with her and told Mrs. Kelly that if she did not divorce William Kelly, King would hire someone to kill her husband. It also emerged through other testimony that King had planned four previous times to have William Kelly murdered, but there was no follow-through.

FLASHBACK: CANDY JUSTICE

On August 12, the first trial ended with a hung jury. When the second trial was held in late September with the prosecution said to have an even better case than before, King pleaded guilty to avoid the gas chamber. His sentence of life in prison turned out to be only 10 years in prison when he was paroled and became a free man. Hardly justice for William Lee Kelly. King got to enjoy 23 more years of freedom, and when he died in 1994, his obituary didn't mention that he was a murderer. When King died, he had 11 grandchildren, 25 great grandchildren and two great-great grandchildren. William Lee Kelly never got to see his little boy grow up.

Someone Shot the President?

Even national news could become a focal point of local coverage. November 22, 1963, was gray and cool in Winona. Bryan's friends and he were talking in groups in front of the school as they waited for the post-lunch bell to ring and bring them back to class. Their senior classmate, Bill Townsend, who always walked up the block to his home for lunch, came running up to them, out of breath and hardly able to talk. "He's been shot! Kennedy's been shot," he gasped. "Kennedy's been shot!" Several people laughed, not really believing him.

President John F. Kennedy, a liberal Democrat, was not popular in the south, especially after the previous year's Ole Miss riots when his administration had forced the university to admit its first Black student, James Meredith. Jokes had often circulated about someone assassinating the president, but most people did not really wish JFK harm. Then another friend ran up. "Bob Chisholm is on the radio saying Kennedy's been shot!" The mood immediately changed. If WONA said the president had been killed, it was true. Someone really did shoot the president.

People scrambled to pull out their transistor radios and turned them up to full volume so all could all hear. "Repeating the bulletin from United Press International, 'Dateline, Dallas, Texas. Three shots were fired at President Kennedy's motorcade today in downtown Dallas.' A later bulletin confirms the president and Texas Governor John Connally were both hit by sniper fire while riding in the presidential limousine. Stay tuned to WONA for more details as they come in."

The students filed silently into the school building, no longer joking, but instead focusing on the details of the impending national tragedy playing from their tiny radios. Classes were forgotten as students and teachers listened intently. As students moved from one classroom to the next, the only sounds in the hallways came from the raspy speakers of miniature transistors. It was real. Bryan was listening along with everyone, but his thoughts were racing ahead. He had to get to the radio station as soon as possible. Mrs. Furness, their history teacher, understood Bryan's angst and impatience and gave him permission to leave class early. By that time, everyone knew Kennedy had died.

Bryan on foot got to WONA in ten minutes. Bob barely looked up from the bulletins he was editing and said to Bryan, "I need you to man the tickers (the UPI and AP news machines) and keep bringing me updated stories." Bob didn't seem the least bit surprised Bryan was there. He just assumed Bryan would come as quickly as possible. For the rest of the day, Bryan monitored the news wires, got Cokes and coffee for everyone, and even read some stories on the air himself. It was his first encounter with what is now ubiquitously known as "breaking news."

Two days later, he was sitting at home on Sunday morning and watching live coverage of assassination suspect Lee Harvey Oswald's transfer from the Dallas County jail. Out of nowhere, a man later identified as Jack Ruby bullied his way through the throng of reporters, stuck a gun in Oswald's stomach, and pulled the trigger. The strange weekend had just gotten bizarre.

After the initial shock, Bryan knew the story had once again been revived. His Mom drove him to the station where he once again manned his post at the UPI and AP machines. Nobody told him he had to be at the station. He just knew that was where he needed to be. That was what Bob did, so that's what Bryan did.

Operator:
"Number please? Are you calling Tommy? He's at Larry's. I'll ring him over there."

If you are younger than 50 or have always lived in a big city, you probably thought the above exchange between a small-town telephone operator and a caller was a joke. It was not. Radio Station WONA shared the Telephone Building in downtown Winona with the workplace of telephone operators, who connected every call in the town, where in the 50s and early 60s, everybody had a three-digit phone number, and nobody had a phone with a rotary dial. If you picked up your phone and a telephone operator did not ask "Number please?" well, you were out of luck. No call for you.

When you picked up the phone at your home or business to call someone and a telephone operator *did* answer, she would say, "Number please?" and you would say something like "968 please." And the ever-efficient operator would put the call through. *Unless* the operator had grown up in Winona and knew everyone in town and had most of their phone numbers memorized and probably had been listening in on a number of private phone conversations that really were not her business.

In that case, something like the words at the top of this page might transpire. According to Bryan, the operator knew that Tommy Tardy was not at home at the moment and wanted to save everyone time and energy by letting him know that Tommy was at Larry

Wilson's house. Without waiting for the go-ahead, the operator kindly connected Bryan to Tommy and Larry.

Like the telephone system, small-town radio was also very personal. It had one major advantage over its big city competition. It was local. Local involvement was the heart of small-town radio in the 1950s and 1960s and the key to its success. The ability to relate directly to the listeners, friends, neighbors, families, employers, employees, teachers, fellow church members and everyone else in town — is what set the little thousand-watt stations apart from, and above, the 50,000-watt behemoths whose signal reached farther, whose music was newer and whose disc jockeys were more experienced.

They were not, however, more famous than announcers in the small towns. Being a DJ in a small town may not have earned you much of a paycheck, but it often earned recognition and maybe even a little respect. People related to local DJs. Everybody knew them and they usually knew the DJ's family. And they had one collective trait. They didn't mind telling the local DJs what they did right and what they did wrong.

"Do you think your Momma would like you playing those records?"

"You really think anybody cares about all that news from Washington?"

Or, "I sure wish you'd play that song for my wife."

Listeners were not shy about sharing their opinions. And if you were smart, you listened to the listeners. Most of the time. However, the advice, "You need to hurry up and get past puberty" was probably not very helpful to the young DJs at the time.

The key to local radio success was being a big part of the lives of the people in the community and always serving as the centerpiece to everything that happened in town. If it was important to the town, WONA covered it.

It wasn't radio as we know it today. No consultants. No preprogrammed music. No automation. It was live…and it was fun. The world of local, small-town radio in 1958 was a challenging adventure for a 12-year-old boy like Bryan, enamored with the magic and captivated by the overwhelming need to be a part of it. For the casual listener, radio was the source of information – from the goings on of the world (albeit briefly told) to local events, funeral notices and even reports of who was in the hospital and who had gone home. Pre HIPPA radio told us pretty much everything we wanted to know about our fellow citizens.

Local commercials plugged grocery specials from Jitney Jungle, Piggly Wiggly, Liberty Cash and Simpson's Cash Grocery ("We have great meats, but don't come between 12:30 and 1:30 because Ethel [the male butcher] will be at lunch and Cecil and Ed don't know anything about cutting steaks").

Piggly Wiggly owner "Chut" Billingsley publicized his specials in a weekly telephone call from Bob or one of the announcers. The one-minute conversation was filled with a recitation of regular prices and always featured specials like, "Hamburger meat, this week only three pounds for a dollar" or "Chickens just 25 cents a pound." Bryan always cringed at those because one of his Saturday jobs was working in the meat market at Piggly Wiggly bagging frozen chickens all morning and grinding hamburger meat the rest of the day.

Weekly cash drawings from Liberty Cash Grocery and, later, Piggly Wiggly, were a regular Saturday afternoon live broadcast. Saturday was the biggest shopping day for local merchants. The chance to win $25 just by registering at the store brought people in to register, and then stay to shop. Bob almost always emceed these events, interviewing the store owner and spectators, young and old, who gathered to hear the name of the lucky winner.

Bryan's earliest memory of being on the radio was the afternoon he was seated on the electric pony outside Liberty Cash while his parents were shopping inside. Bob asked Bryan and his friends what they would do if their parents won the upcoming drawing. Bryan's brilliant ad-lib answer, "I'd faint," was the opening line to his broadcast career. Bob must have been impressed, because a few years later he allowed Bryan to conduct the weekly drawing from Piggly Wiggly.

Back then, there was the music – not rap, not country, not soul, not that new rock and roll noise – just that pleasant MOR (Middle of the Road) stuff everyone liked. You could hear Mantovani, Perry Como, Ray Conniff, Patti Page, Dean Martin and if you were in a raucous mood, Spike Jones.

WONA was not on the air 24 hours a day like some big city stations. Sign-on and sign-off times varied by the time of year. WONA was a "daytimer," a low power, 1,000-watt station that was only licensed to operate from sunrise until sunset.

To make things easier, the FCC (Federal Communications Commission) published specific sign-on and sign-off times for each day of the year. In the summer, extended daylight meant longer program hours. In the winter, the station went on the air much later and signed off far earlier. The times were inviable. Signing on one minute earlier or getting off even 30 seconds too late meant the possibility of a fine by the FCC.

The only real competition in the fifties and sixties came from WHBQ radio in Memphis in the daytime, and WLS in Chicago at night. And this was strictly for teenagers. WHBQ was the number one rock station in Memphis, 125 miles away. On a good weather day, it had enough power to reach Winona, allowing teens to listen to Elvis, Pat Boone, the Everly Brothers, and even Chuck Berry and Little Richard.

WLS in Chicago was known as a "Clear Channel" station. After sundown, it was the only radio station in the entire country on its assigned frequency (890 kilocycles) and thus had the power to reach far across the nation without interference.

Teenagers took their transistor radios to bed with them at night and listened through the static to the nighttime antics of Dick Biondi as he played their music, read zany commercials and took calls from listeners. Winonians were all thrilled one night when Biondi aired a call from Winona as Bob Graves, using his best reporter's voice, described Peanut Holmes' death-defying and probable world-record 30-minute tumble in a laundromat dryer. The call was one of the headlines the next morning on WONA's Morning Edition of the News. It may have aired across the nation, but it was still our local news.

The Winona Times weekly newspaper could have been a competitor to WONA. Forged by a friendship and a mutual respect between Bob Chisholm and Times editor Hembree Brandon, the two media sources instead became allies that offered complementary coverage of local events. Bob and Hembree often worked together on major news stories, especially those involving City Hall, in order to cover them completely. Separately, they were formidable. Together, Bob and Hembree were force majeure. Given the nature of small-town media, it would be easy to dismiss the duo as mediocre newsmen.

While it is true their respective outlets delivered stories about bridge clubs, garden clubs, Rotary and Lions clubs and the election of Mr. and Miss Winona High School, these stories were accurate and well-written. This was the news people **wanted** to hear.

What set these men apart was their coverage also of the news people **needed** to hear. Both were men of integrity. Both were excellent writers. And both were relentless in their pursuit of fair and accurate reporting.

Riding on the City of New Orleans

Candy and her dad were talking in his tiny office at the radio station when Bob stopped mid-sentence and smiled affectionately at the sound coming from the railroad tracks that run through downtown Winona.

"It's *The City*," he said fondly.

Most people in Winona called it by its full name, "The City of New Orleans" or simply "the train," but to Bob Chisholm it was always "*The City*." In 1947, the City of New Orleans had been introduced by the Illinois Central Railroad as a daytime all-coach train duo with the Panama Limited, an overnight all Pullman train, both sharing the same route, which created the longest daylight run in the United States. *The City* stopped twice a day in Winona on its run from New Orleans to Chicago and back again.

The Panama Limited, *The City's* snooty older brother, had been operating as a passenger train since 1911 and was the flagship train of the Illinois Central Railroad. It was named for the Panama Canal, which was three years from completion in 1911. There was no real connection and the Panama Limited didn't go anywhere near the canal.

Besides being older than the City of New Orleans, the Panama Limited could also brag about being "all-Pullman," which meant that it was made up of sleeping cars only — no coach passengers, The City of New Orleans, when Amtrak took over all U.S. passenger train service in 1971, had a diesel locomotive pulling new light-weight coach cars that had an average speed of 60 miles per hour and could go as fast as 100 miles per hour. It had an excellent dining car, but it could not compare to the luxurious meals on the Panama Limited, which had a top-flight culinary staff. Multi-course meals included creole fare and lobster, steak, wine and cocktails. In 1967, the Panama Limited added coach service for the first time in 50 years.

Few people from Winona traveled on the Panama Limited because that train didn't stop in Winona. Hank Holmes, a Winona native and retired executive director of the Mississippi Department of Archives and History, was a seasoned train traveler at an early age, riding between New Orleans and Winona on the City of New Orleans by himself as a kid.

One of Hank's relatives found a way around the problem of the Panama Limited not stopping in Winona.

"An aunt from New Orleans would ride the Panama Limited from NOLA, sitting in the end club car because the Panama Limited was all Pullman, and she would get off at Grenada where we would pick her up and drive her to Winona."

Every Tuesday in the 1950s and early 1960s, cattle buyers from Illinois and Missouri arrived by train in Winona to take part in the livestock auction. Because the buyers arrived very early, they were fed a big southern breakfast cooked by Morris Graves, the wife of Harry Graves, the owner of the livestock barn, and several other women like Montee Blaylock, who along with her husband Leo worked for the Graves family for many years. In fact, the Blaylocks are buried beside Morris and Harry Graves. Harry's grandson, Bob

Graves, who often drove the cattle buyers to and from the train station, recalls the shock he and others experienced when a buyer arrived not by train but flying his own plane to Winona.

For those who didn't ride on the train regularly, the City of New Orleans still produced excitement of the small-town variety. Phyllis Townsend Ward, who grew up in Winona and now lives in Dallas, has many happy memories of her mother, Betty Townsend, and Phyllis's paternal grandmother "Edily" taking 5-year-old Phyllis and her 8-year-old brother Charlie to the depot to watch passengers get on and off the train at Winona. The Townsends weren't going anywhere, but it was somehow exciting for the children to see others going and coming on the train.

"My first out of town trip alone was on the City of New Orleans to go visit Grandmother in Memphis," Phyllis recalled. "I was 12 and thought I was a grown up, but I ate lifesavers all the way like the kid I was. Grandmother met me at the Memphis train station and took me to Pappy & Jimmy's to eat."

Many years later, Phyllis, Hank and Candy would travel on the City of New Orleans every December to spend a few days in New Orleans, a ritual they still follow. While there, they tell anyone who will listen (cab drivers, waiters, desk clerks) that they are celebrating 65 years of friendship. These friends since childhood love the fine dining and other joys of New Orleans, but they agree that the train trip is the real destination.

A trip from Memphis to NOLA lost some of its Americana charm in 1995 when Amtrak rerouted the train through the flat, barren Mississippi Delta between Memphis and Jackson. Five towns lost passenger train service — Batesville, Grenada, Durant, Canton and Winona. It was a sad day for Winona train lovers. And many train travelers at night find that the endless darkness of the Delta without towns and lights can be very disorienting. However, it gives the passengers an understanding of the City of New Orleans lyrics that speak of the "Mississippi darkness rolling down to the sea."

A few years ago, Candy and Phyllis, who is a second mother to Candy's children, took *The City* to New Orleans with Candy's children and their spouses and young children. They found themselves traveling between Memphis and New Orleans with a group of musicians, who spent the whole trip singing and playing instruments in the observation car, not paid, just for fun.

One of the musicians was Richard Leigh, who wrote "Don't It Make My Brown Eyes Blue," for which he won a Grammy award in 1978. When the group struck up the song "City of New Orleans," it was quite a thrill for all their listeners, many of whom sang along, as they rode their "magic carpets made of steel." With or without musicians on the train, it is not uncommon for south-bound passengers, as they approach the Crescent City in midafternoon, to spontaneously sing "City of New Orleans." Some even get up and dance in the aisles.

When Candy and family got back to Memphis, it was late at night but Sylvia, who was four at the time, had, along with her cousins, Matthew and Betty, fallen in love with train travel. When they drove away from the Memphis train station, Sylvia burst into tears saying, "I don't want to leave my train!"

"Good night, America, how are you? Don't you know me? I'm your native son! I'm the train they call the City of New Orleans. I'll be gone 500 miles when the day is done."

Because Arlo Guthrie made that song famous, many people think he wrote it. But it was written by Steve Goodman, who had a small but loyal following in his hometown of Chicago. He was at the Quiet Knight bar when Arlo Guthrie, already a famous entertainer, happened to be there. Steve asked Arlo if he could play one of his songs for him. Guthrie was not thrilled about having to listen to a would-be "star" but agreed to listen to Steve play and sing his song if Steve bought him a beer and Arlo only had to listen long enough to finish drinking the beer.

Steve Goodman played and sang "City of New Orleans" and Guthrie liked it so much, he asked if he could record the song. Arlo Guthrie's version of the song became a Top 20 hit in 1972, and Steve Goodman got enough money and artistic success from that song that he was able to make a full-time career out of music.

This fairy tale had one big hitch, however. Steve Goodman had been plagued with fatigue and was diagnosed with leukemia at the age of 20. Still, Steve married and they had three daughters, and he had a rewarding recording career. But according to his wife, he always knew he was living on borrowed time. He died in the emergency room of a Seattle hospital when he was 36.

Steve's wife Nancy wrote this in the liner notes of his posthumous collection "No Big Surprise":

"Basically, Steve was exactly who he appeared to be: an ambitious, well-adjusted man from a loving, middle-class Jewish home in the Chicago suburbs, whose life and talent were directed by the physical pain and time constraints of a fatal disease which he kept at bay, at times, seemingly by willpower alone…Steve wanted to live as normal a life as possible, only he had to live it as fast as he could…He extracted meaning from the mundane."

Steve wrote and performed several humorous songs about his

long-suffering hometown baseball team, including: "When the Cubs Go Marching In," "Go, Cubs, Go" and "A Dying Cubs Fan's Last Request."

Steve Goodman just missed by four days getting to know that his Cubs clinched the National League East division title for the first time ever. At the conclusion of every home-game win, the Chicago Cubs play and fans sing "Go, Cubs, Go." In 1988, some of Steve Goodman's ashes were scattered at the Cubs' Wrigley Field. Many of Steve's friends and fans thought "City of New Orleans" was more about Steve's impending death than about the death of a train, or maybe it was both.

FLASH BACK: BRYAN COTTINGHAM

I have loved trains for as long as I can remember. When I was 10 years old, we lived just a few hundred yards from the train depot. I vividly remember the haunting whistle of a passenger train as it slipped into Winona for its midnight stop.

I think I subconsciously lay awake every night until I heard that whistle and the reassuring sound of the train lumbering to a momentary stop. I still remember the hiss of escaping compressed air and the squeal of the brakes enveloped in that wonderful diesel smell that wafted down to our house.

Even today, those sounds and smells take me back to that wonderful time growing up in a small southern town. Sometimes passengers got on or off the train, but it often stopped only long enough to pick up mail, drop off packages and resume its quiet journey through the Mississippi darkness.

The train depot stands on the edge of Front Street, the home of so many downtown businesses. Tardy Furniture, White's Auto Supplies, Liberty Cash, Walker's Five and Dime, Gordon's

**Simpson's Cash Grocery is typical of the stores in Winona.
Photo courtesy of Edward Simpson III**

Department Store, King's Sporting Goods, Jackson's, Dacus Furniture, the Winona Theater and Simpson's Cash Grocery were just some of the locally owned businesses that served the 5,000 residents every day. I spent many hours as a young boy at Simpson's, my grandfather's "Mom and Pop" grocery later run by two of my uncles.

Granddaddy used to meet the early freight train at 5 a.m. every day to pick out fresh flowers and plants to sell in his store located less than 200 yards from the depot. Sometimes he loaded crates of his self-raised squab, a delicacy iced down and destined for restaurants around the south. In a small town, he had to be resourceful to make a living and support himself, my grandmother and their seven children. Other merchants often met the train for early morning packages and urgently needed supplies. They didn't have the luxury of personal deliveries from FedEx, UPS or Amazon.

For a simple reason. None of them existed. Deliveries were made to the Railway Express office at the north end of the depot and picked up by the addressees. I still remember the giant, green, rolling hand carts that carried freight inside from the train to the office.

During my senior year of high school, I used to spend time at the train depot. My girlfriend Dianne's father, Henry Milner, was the Station Master on the 3-11 shift.

I would sit in his office, marveling at his dexterity with the telegraph key as the fast-moving dashes, dots and clicks conveyed and received information to and from the masters of train stations up and down the line. My Boy Scout Morse Code merit badge was no match for the speed, complexity and experience of the telegraphers. I watched as he sold tickets, gathered the outgoing mail and prepared the incoming mail for delivery to the post office a few blocks away.

The primitive 2-way communication system with the engineers and conductors kept him abreast of arrivals and delays along the rails. It wasn't quite as fascinating as radio, but it was wonderful entertainment. Some 50 years later, I had the chance to visit with Dianne and reminisce about her father as we ate at a restaurant table in the refurbished depot. We were sitting at a table located right where her father's desk had sat in the early 60s. I love nostalgia.

The Winona depot is even mentioned in the story of the "heroic" death of famed engineer Casey Jones in a horrific crash near Vaughn, Mississippi. According to the official report, Jones left Memphis about 1 a.m. on April 30, 1900, about 75 minutes behind schedule. The engineer, proud of his on-time record, reportedly drove the train at excessive speeds in order to make up for the late start. He made up 15 minutes of that time as he sped from Grenada (25 miles away) and roared through Winona at two o'clock in the morning. It has always been fascinating to me that Jones, who caused the fatal crash in his reckless attempt to make up time, has always been lauded as the heroic engineer who died in the wreck.

FLASHBACK: BRYAN COTTINGHAM

I was 14 years old when I took my first train ride. To say it was memorable is a classic understatement. I had read an article about Congressional pages in our Weekly Reader magazine in school and was intrigued by their duties. High school students (only boys were allowed in 1961) worked in the Capitol building in Washington, delivering messages and running errands for members of the Senate and the House of Representatives. With a bit of youthful bravado, no doubt fueled by three years of exposure to radio and to Bob Chisholm, I wrote Congressman Jamie Whitten, the representative for our district, and boldly asked for an appointment as a page. I received an immediate reply thanking me for my interest, but noting that I might be a little young for the job since I would be somewhat on my own while living in Washington, D.C.

I swallowed my disappointment but made a mental note to try again next year – and the next and the next if it was necessary. It wasn't. Two months later, my parents showed up at the Piggly Wiggly where I was working after school and handed me a very official looking letter from the Congressman. (They admitted later they were so titillated by the official Congressional seal that they had steamed the letter open and read it). After a perfunctory greeting, the Congressman got to the point. His May appointment had withdrawn, so he had an extra opening to fill. Was I interested, even with just three week's notice? Well, yeah! And, by the way, we'll pay you $365 for the month.

Winona train station. Photo courtesy Bain Hughes.

The next three weeks were a frenzy of preparation. I had to make arrangements to pick up future assignments from my teachers. After all, I was going to be going to school in a classroom located in the Library of Congress. Mom and Dad took me to the Bank of Winona, where I successfully applied for my first loan to cover buying the required blue suit and having enough money to pay for lodging in a private boarding house for pages ($180 for the month, including one meal a day), and enough spending money for the month. The loan was to be paid back from the entirety of my $365 check, but who cared? I was going to stand on the floor of Congress!

Looking back, it's interesting my parents never raised an objection. Congressman Whitten's office had assured them I would be well supervised during work hours and that the boarding house had an excellent reputation. Washington, of course, was much safer in 1961 than it is now. This also was not the first time I had travelled without them. The year before, I had taken a two-week bus tour through the west and then camped for a week at the National Boy Scout Jamboree in Colorado Springs.

My parents trusted me to make good decisions based on my upbringing in Winona and knew this would be the adventure of a lifetime for me. Still, I know they must have worried about me while I was gone. Today, I can't imagine the enormity of being 14 years old and living and working in a strange city a thousand miles from home. At the time, however, the idea seemed perfectly normal.

After a fortnight plus of frantically scurrying around, it was time for me to board the train for my trip to Washington – by myself. There were no morning passenger trains passing through Winona, so my parents drove me two hours to the train station in Memphis. Call it the innocence of youth, but I wasn't nervous about the somewhat solo adventure that faced me for the next month. I was just excited to be going.

The train lurched forward as I waved goodbye, armed with enough reading material and sandwiches to sustain me for the planned eight-hour trip. I was so mesmerized by the changing scenery that I didn't even pick up the books. The trees, rivers and cities – big and small – unfolded in front of me, accompanied by the soothing clatter of the wheels on steel rails.

I wandered from car to car, especially enjoying the noisy passages between compartments. Even though I had food with me, I splurged $3 on my first club sandwich, appropriately served with a Coke in the club car.

Then, the plan suddenly changed as we entered Virginia. Another train was stalled on the tracks ahead of us and we had to wait. And we had to wait. And we had to wait. Five hours later, the track was cleared, and we restarted the journey.

By the time we crept into Washington's Union Station, it was 11 o'clock at night and the rain was pouring down. I stood alone with my suitcase in the middle of the biggest train station I had ever seen and looked around for the taxi stand I had been told to find when I arrived. I got a cab as instructed and handed the driver the address of the boarding house, 101 5th Street N.E. That was the sum total of my information.

There was no way I could call and warn the owner of the boarding house, the sweet and generous Mrs. Smith, that I would be late. The driver whisked me through the rain-soaked streets of Washington to my destination.

We passed the Supreme Court building, the Capitol building where I would be working and the Library of Congress where I would be studying. All were grandly lit up and shone through the heavy rain. We turned left in front of the Capitol and moved along the trolley tracks past the Shakespeare Library to the boarding house. It was midnight when we pulled up to a connected row of houses.

A single porch light was shining at 101 5th Street when the driver opened the trunk, handed me my suitcase…and drove off, leaving the 14-year-old kid from Winona standing in the rain, illuminated by a street light half a block away. I timidly walked up the steps and rang the doorbell, my bravado momentarily shaken. Almost immediately, the door flew open, and the obviously relieved Mrs. Smith enveloped me with a tight hug exclaiming, "I am SO glad to see you. Are you OK? What happened? I'm so happy you're here. Are you hungry? Is everything OK? Have you called your parents? I am so happy to see you!"

I think she was happy to see me. I was certainly glad to see her. And this was just the beginning of the adventure. The next month was filled with a whirlwind of new experiences, people and discoveries. In my free time, I explored every historical nook, cranny and building in Washington.

I don't think I missed anything. I roamed the eclectic buildings of the Smithsonian Institution for hours on end, gazed at the gigantic dinosaurs, stared at paintings I had only read about, stood in awe beneath the plane piloted by the Wright Brothers in their historic first flight and tried to imagine the loneliness of Lindbergh as I looked up at the *Spirit of St. Louis* hanging from the ceiling. I wandered through the graves of Arlington Cemetery in a light mist, having no idea that just two years from then, the young president I was soon to encounter would also lie at rest.

Taking the trolley to the Library of Congress for school became a common daily occurrence. Each morning after classes, I walked across the street and casually climbed the steps of the Capitol to go to work, where I routinely walked through the history of our country all day long.

I met Speaker of the House Sam Rayburn, Vice-President (soon to be president) Lyndon Johnson, as well as congressmen and senators we had read about in social studies.

The House Minority Whip often wandered to the rear of the chamber and sat with us to discuss history and the workings of the government. He asked us to call him Gerry. The future president of the United States, Gerald Ford, was our buddy. I shook the hand of Alan Shepard and the other six original Mercury astronauts just days after his historic flight as the first American in space.

A week later, another page and I opened the door to the House chambers as John F. Kennedy strode to the dais and challenged Americans to "Put a man on the moon by the end of the decade." As the youngest page in the House or Senate at the time, I was probably more awed than the others. In fact, I discovered later I was one of the youngest pages ever to work in Congress. But for some reason, it all just seemed natural.

I don't remember anything about the train ride home. All I know is that I took a cab to Union Station (by then, I was a taxi veteran), boarded the train and arrived on time in Memphis. My head and heart were too full to even notice the blurred scenery as we passed through the countryside. All in all, though, I would have to say the round trip was one hell of a first train ride.

Les Nabors, who worked a daily board shift, was also a Methodist minister.
Below, the control panel for WONA
Photo courtesy Candy Chisholm

Chapter 4

Antics and Pranks

Bryan was proud to be working at WONA and serious about his work there, but he was also in awe of his older fellow announcers. He knew of Ed Forsythe because Ed was the drummer for The Downbeats, a popular dance band that had formed at Ole Miss and played around the South. Ed was probably the hippest of the jocks. After all, he was a musician and a college boy — he had the most fun on the air. Ed is the one who taught Bryan some of the practical jokes that were common in live radio.

Once, Bryan was reading a live commercial — which radio people called "spots" — when Ed walked in with a lighter and set fire to the top of Bryan's script. Because it was live, Bryan had to read faster and faster to stay ahead of the advancing flames.

Ed also set traps for the other announcers. The microphone for the control console (the board) was on a long, flexible tube that some people would move up or down as they stood or sat at the board. When an announcer went outside the control room to pull copy from the UPI machine, Ed would reposition the mic.

Waiting until the last minute to rush into the control room as a record ended, the DJ would open the mic switch and start talking, only to discover the mic was sticking straight up in the air and that he sounded like he was talking in a well.

Usually, he would keep talking as he reached up and hurriedly pulled the mic down to his face. It made for an interesting sound on the air.

Les Nabors was the young Methodist circuit preacher in the Winona area. Circuit preaching didn't pay too well so Les helped feed his family by working part-time at WONA. A flaming redhead, Les was well liked by everyone at the station. He had a great voice and is one of the nicest people you will ever know. Les usually signed the station on in the mornings. He was not a morning person and would usually come in half-awake to start his shift. A bit of logistical information is needed here.

Like most small radio stations in the early 60s, the control room had two 16" record turntables, one on either side of the board. While a record was playing on one turntable, the announcer would cue (prepare) a record on the other side. Since records came with different speeds, each turntable could be adjusted to play at speeds of $33^{1/3}$, 45 or 78 revolutions per minute (rpm). WONA's albums all played at $33^{1/3}$. When Ed Forsythe would sign off in the evening, he would turn both turntables to 78 rpm.

The next morning, a sleepy Les Nabors would come in, cue up his first two records and sign on. As soon as he started playing his first song, Les and the listeners would hear a very sped up chipmunk sounding recording. Les would quickly grab the switch and change the turntable from 78 rpm to $33^{1/3}$, making a singer sound as if he were on Quaaludes. It was a very interesting experience for the listeners, and for the now wide-awake DJ.

To this day, Les, now a retired and still respected Methodist minister, denies his most famous on-the-air gaffe. He was eating lunch while a taped program was airing. As would sometimes happen, the tape broke. Rather than face dead air while he restrung the tape and got it going again, Les grabbed a record, quickly cued it up, started playing it and opened the mic. "We are experiencing technical difficulties," he informed the audience. "While we repair them, we invite you to enjoy a short *intercourse* of music." Live radio was so much fun.

Maurice Gooch gave Bryan his first chance to actually function at the board as a real announcer. Gooch was the chief engineer and also took shifts as an announcer. He took Bryan under his wing and worked with him more than any of the others. The more experienced jocks were all good to the younger guys like Bryan, but Maurice was his special buddy.

Bryan showed up earlier than usual one weekend morning for his unofficial, unscheduled and unpaid shift as an observer. The evening before, Gooch had told Bryan he was having some trouble with the transmitter and wasn't sure it was going to turn on the next morning. Bryan fantasized a scenario where Gooch would have to drive 10 minutes out to the transmitter in the early morning, jiggle some wires, twist some tubes and then call and say, "put her on the air, Bryan!" Bryan decided he was going to be there just in case that did happen. Guess what? The transmitter wouldn't turn on the next morning, Maurice drove 10 minutes to get to the site, jiggled some wires, twisted some tubes and called Bryan at the station. "Put her on the air, Bryan. I need to stay here and make sure everything is okay."

FLASHBACK: BRYAN COTTINGHAM

Acting like the veteran I wasn't, I hung up the phone, keyed the mic and started talking. "Good Morning," I read from the sign-on script, "This is WONA, Winona, Mississippi, beginning another broadcast day…" I finished the sign-on, turned off the mic and started the first record (I had already checked the sign-on script, pulled some records and cued up the first song. Never be caught off guard by your fantasies). For some reason, Bob, who was usually the first to arrive seven days a week, wasn't there. I still wonder if Bob was surprised by my being on the air or if he already knew it was going to happen. He never said anything, and I never asked him.

When Gooch got back to the station, he said he had some things he needed to do to make sure the transmitter was okay and asked me if I minded staying on the air for a while. Are you kidding? How about all day? I was officially a Disc Jockey (I believe you should always capitalize exotic titles). Looking back, I think the transmitter problem was a ploy to give me a chance to go on the air. I'll never ask. Hey, it's MY fantasy. And Gooch is my friend.

OOPS!!!!

"We didn't have breakfast without Bob Chisholm," said Carole Watts Graves, whose dad, Fred Watts, was mayor of Winona for eight years and the beloved press-box voice of the Winona Tigers for many, many years.

Well, maybe the Watts family and almost every other family in Winona had breakfast with Bob Chisholm, but the Chisholm family always had an empty chair at the breakfast table. But Carol and Candy didn't mind because they were proud of the work he was doing for their town with his 7 a.m. newscast.

Lunch was a different thing. The little kitchen in the Chisholm house had a table just big enough for the three of them to eat lunch together some days. Candy usually came home from school for lunch rather than eat in the school cafeteria. If Bob had an announcer on duty he could trust, he would leave the 15-minute noon news — mostly national news from United Press International — in that trusted person's hands, and he'd come home to eat a quick sandwich with his family.

And the radio in the kitchen was always on, so he could keep an eye on WONA from a few blocks away. There was little or no lunch conversation because they were all listening to the news, but not because they needed to know what was going on in the world — after all, the Chisholms took two newspapers a day, including the *Memphis Press-Scimitar*, which Candy would go on to report for from 1973-1983, watched TV news at night, Carol had her own daily news and music show and the family talked about news all the time. They listened to every word spoken on WONA during lunch because sometimes Bob came home to eat even when there was *not* a trusted announcer on duty.

On those days, they were holding their collective breath that the announcer would not make an embarrassing mistake on the air. On a *good* day, it was a little tense but nothing bad happened. On a *bad* day, Bob would explode over some mispronunciation or exercise of bad judgment by the announcer. He never accepted mediocrity, but sometimes —because of circumstances — he had to tolerate it.

The malapropos were the ones that were hard for Candy not to giggle about. But her dad never found them funny until many years had passed. Like the day the announcer was supposed to say that during a riot in a third world country, peasants (poor people) were looting and burning, but the announcer *actually* said that pheasants (birds) were looting and burning. What a difference one letter can make.

Another time, their lunch was disrupted by an announcer who said that the president had called congressional leaders to the White House on Sunday for an emergency meeting. The young announcer was *supposed* to say, "However, Senator George Romney, a devout Mormon, did not attend because he doesn't work on Sunday." What the announcer *actually* said on the air was, "However, Senator

George Romney, a devout moron, did not attend because he doesn't work on Sunday." Again, what a difference one letter can make.

Those kind of mistakes Bob considered inexcusable, embarrassing and a sign of ignorance. But the unprofessional things that some young announcers did intentionally in a misguided attempt to be funny, Bob considered unforgiveable.

Winona is in Montgomery County, which was a dry county then, meaning alcoholic beverages could not be legally sold there. The proponents of making Montgomery a wet county managed to get the issue on the ballot, and both sides were buying advertising in the *Winona Times* and on WONA.

WONA and the *Winona Times*, of course, were neutral and selling advertising to both sides. It was a very sensitive, hotly contested issue that had to be handled carefully by the station. One day at lunchtime, an announcer did as he was supposed to and played a paid pre-recorded message from the Montgomery County Ministerial Association urging citizens to vote against the evils of legal alcohol. Then when the pre-recorded message was over, the young announcer, trying to be funny, hiccupped on the air and in a drunken voice said, "I'll drink to that!" Nobody remembers if Bob fired the kid, but Bob did not finish his lunch. He left the house like he had been shot from a cannon.

"That young announcer was NOT me," Bryan says adamantly. Small town radio is the training ground for most announcers. It's the place you go to learn and to make your mistakes with a smaller audience. That's the theory. Some people, however, are just not cut out for radio at any level. Some were phantom ships that passed in the night and were quickly forgotten. Some never got out of port, and some scuttled themselves while they were still in dry dock. Bob was a stickler for accuracy, whether it was a news fact or the correct pronunciation of a word. If you were talking on the radio, you pronounced words correctly. Well, at least most announcers did.

One neophyte, whose career could be measured by the life expectancy of a fruit fly, talked himself out of a job rather quickly. While reading a story on the air about a person accused of a crime, he referred to the man as having been *INDICATED* by a grand jury. He also read a story about aid to *INDIGNANT* people.

Bryan told him he was sure they were not happy about being poor but were merely indigent. That young announcer didn't take too well to being corrected, even by Bob. The last straw came when he aired a story about a giant "uhTOM" smasher (atom smasher). When Bob tried to (somewhat) gently point out the error, he was met with unrighteous indignation. "You're wrong, "uhTOM" is spelled a-t-o-m. The word you are saying is spelled a-d-o-m." Exit stage left.

Another short termer was a dedicated rip and reader. That's someone who rips the stories off the wire machines and doesn't bother looking at them before reading them on the air for the first time. This is NOT a good idea. Every newscast sounded like amateur night as he struggled through foreign names and read stories with no comprehension. The last straw came one afternoon when he asked Bryan if he could come in and do the 3 o'clock newscast so the announcer could leave early for a doctor's appointment.

Bryan agreed but asked him to put together the newscast since he could not get to the station until a few minutes before 3 o'clock. When Bryan got to the station, the erstwhile announcer tossed him a pile of UPI stories that had been ripped from the machine and not edited or put together in any order. "I ran out of time," he yelled over his shoulder as he exited through the control room door. Bryan started reading the first story on the air. It turned out to be what is today called a breaking news story. He read the bulletin and then read two unrelated stories. The next item was an "update" that had actually been sent before the first story Bryan had already read. He ended up giving several updates, all out of sequence. As soon as Bryan finished the newscast, Bob came in and asked what was going on. When Bryan explained the situation to him, Bob was livid, not at Bryan, but at the person who put the station and him in that embarrassing position. Bob called the now ex-announcer and told him not to report for his next scheduled shift.

No one remembers the name of the young man who was surely Bob's least favorite short-term announcer. He called himself "The Wild, Wild Child" on the air. And he was. Bob was desperate to find an announcer. All his announcers had either left or turned in their notice in the fall of 1966. Bryan was in college in Memphis at the time, studying radio and television, when he got a pleading call from Bob, asking him if he would consider taking a semester off and coming down to work at the station.

Bob said the hours would be long because the two of them would be the only on-the-air people to cover a 14-hour-a-day, 7-day-a-week schedule. When you are 20 years old and in love with radio, you don't have to hesitate even for a moment when you get that offer. Bryan immediately said yes, although his fiancé and later ex-wife was not happy about that answer.

Bob and Bryan split the duties. Bryan did all the on-air work and Bob did everything else – managing the station, selling ads, gathering and writing the news and trying to find more announcers. To quote only half of Dickens' introduction to *A Tale of Two Cities*, "It was the best of times" for Bryan, who was living a young radio man's dream, on the air 14 hours a day, doing what he had always wanted to do. Youth, innocence and enthusiasm have a way of protecting us.

The Wild, Wild Child came into their lives a couple of months later. To be honest, he invaded their lives. Bob was at his wit's end. He had to find announcers before they both collapsed from exhaustion. WWC was tall, gaunt, smoked incessantly and had wild, curly blonde hair. He also had what Bob and Bryan later realized was a semi-crazed look in his eyes.

This was probably the last time Bob ever hired an announcer sight, or sound, unseen. Bob and Bryan listened together as WWC opened the mic and spoke his first words on WONA. It wasn't a debut. It was a hostage situation. Bob and Bryan looked at each other in disbelief as an almost unintelligible screech came across the airwaves. About the only thing they could really understand was that he was the Wild, Wild Child, and he was going to bring real music and entertainment to the lucky people of Winona, Mississippi.

Bob sent Bryan running into the control room to defuse the situation. As Bryan burst into the control room, he was greeted by the spectacle of WWC smoking furiously, screaming and gesturing as his left leg furiously pumped up and down. Then he finished his spiel and started a record,

Bryan suggested that this was a nice, small Mississippi town, and he might want to tone down just a little bit. Bryan returned to Bob's office just in time to hear a repeat of his initial assault. Bob looked at Bryan and said, "This ain't gonna work." He decided he was going to give him a couple of days and then fire him. Then Bob said to Bryan, "I need to ask you a favor. Can he stay with you tonight? He doesn't have a place to stay. I promise it will just be for one night." Bryan was living in a rented room across the tracks from the station with only one double bed but agreed.

The next day, halfway through his shift, WWC's voice gave out and Bryan (mercifully) had to take over the newcomer's shift. When WWC went to the doctor, he was told he had a very bad case of strep throat and would have to stay in the hospital for a few days. Bob's plan to fire him went right out the window, only to be replaced by a four-day hospital bill, which the station paid.

There was no way Bob was going to fire a guy with no money while he was in the hospital. He waited until the boy's parents came and took him home from the hospital. Then he fired him. By tacit agreement, Bob and Bryan never talked about the Wild, Wild Child again.

Like any young beginner, Bryan had a few of his own on-air gaffes. Bob forgave him when he stumbled over a story and referred to President Eisenhower's *ball* bladder surgery. He even chuckled a bit when some people complained about Bryan referring to a basketball player as "a real stud horse."

Because he knew Bryan was learning and because he knew he was a dedicated hard worker, Bob had almost infinite patience with him. **Almost** infinite patience. In a small town you usually have a few business owners who like to do their own commercials. Some do a good job, and some should know better. Chut Billingsley owned the local Piggly Wiggly supermarket and did a weekly phone call to list the specials of the week. Chut was entertaining and articulate — people looked forward to these phone call visits.

Not so a local used car dealer. His commercials were boisterous and irritating, but he insisted on doing them himself. He was also known in town to be, shall we delicately say, a heavy imbiber. Everyone in town knew this. Well, almost everyone. Bryan obviously was not in on the "secret," a fact that became relevant one afternoon. At the end of one of his recorded commercials, the dealer wanted to let people know he had a lot of cars to sell. His closing line was, "Come out and see us. We're loaded."

Bryan opened the mic and cleverly and naively ad-libbed, "I bet you are." Before he could even close the mic, Bryan heard a scream from Bob's office. "Nooooo!" He came running into the control room and bellowed (few people had ever heard Bob bellow before. It was a scary sound.) "Don't EVER say that again. Everyone knows he's a drunk!" Bryan claims that was the only time in all the years he knew Bob that he had been on the receiving end of Bob's wrath. Fortunately, the car dealer heard Bryan's comment and thought it was funny. After that, he closed all his commercials with the tag line, "Come out and see us. We're loaded."

FLASHBACK: BRYAN COTTINGHAM

With all his experience, his preparation and his attention to detail, you would think Bob never made mistakes on the air. Not so. Even Bob was not immune to error. I was in the control room one morning and heard this classic. Bob and some of the city officials were usually not on good terms. Actually, that's an understatement. They *hated* Bob. They resented his (accurate) reporting about some of their behind-the-scenes maneuvering.

This particular morning, Bob was delivering the Morning Edition of the News, the award-winning newscast he always wrote himself and teased the upcoming segment featuring his monthly coverage of the meeting of the mayor and board of aldermen.

"Stay tuned, because after this commercial break, I'll be back with my monthly report from *Shitty* Hall." Unfortunately, he made the error worse by quickly correcting himself. What the listeners heard was, "… I'll be back with my report from *Shitty City Hall.*" The cascade of phone calls following the story was evenly split between those who just wanted to point out the error and those who agreed with him.

Bob had one more embarrassing moment, this time off the air. When I started working at the station, you simply had to send in an application to get a license to be on the air. A couple of years into my teenage career, the FCC changed the rules and started requiring announcers to take a test to get a third-class radio-telephone license with a broadcast endorsement.

Bob ordered a copy of the study book, which I diligently read. When I gave Bob the book to study, my offer was nonchalantly dismissed. "I'm not worried about the test," Bob said. "I've been in radio a long time. I doubt they would ask something I haven't experienced." *Yep, you already know where this is going.*

The two of us drove to Memphis together (a two-hour trip) and took the test. A couple of weeks later the results came to the station. I had passed the test, but Bob had failed. That may be the only time anyone saw Bob openly embarrassed. He sheepishly retrieved the book and carefully studied it until he passed the test. Bob and I never talked about the incident again. At least Bob didn't.

Top Pop Rock Jock on WONA

Although WONA was primarily a radio station aimed at adults and played music adults liked, Bob carved out a place on weekday afternoons and on Saturdays for rock 'n roll — to the delight of local teenagers. Several high school students over the years were disc jockeys on those programs, but perhaps the one with the greatest flare was Macy B. Hart, known as the Top Pop Rock Jock.

Macy began his "career" at age 8 working for $5 a day as a salesman in the bargain basement of his family's store, Schneider's Department Store, in downtown Winona. Another clothing store,

Smart Shop, was the only business separating Schneider's from the Telephone Building. WONA rented space for its business office and studios "high atop the lovely Telephone Building," as Bob Chisholm liked to joke.

Macy was quite the entrepreneur around town — or as he likes to jokingly say, he was an "entre manure." As a Boy Scout, with the rank of Eagle, he served as a "Den Chief" for a Cub Scout Troop in Winona. Mrs. Inez Kennedy was the Den Mother. He said it was a great experience.

He organized a fundraiser for the Scouts, a hotdog stand outside the Courthouse. In exchange for WONA promoting the Scout's stand, Macy made a deal with Bob to provide Scout runners with the latest vote totals between the Courthouse and WONA on local election nights.

In high school, Macy became a part-time music promoter — along with friends Putt Crull, Alan Wilson, Eddie Barnes, Charlie Townsend, Bob Hammond, Phillip Felts and others. They booked such popular dance bands as Cozzy Corley and the Blue Gardenias Show Band, The Gants and The Counts. The guys all chipped in $25 each to pay for promotional posters, to rent space and pay the band. And the young Winona promoters made $25 to $50, and their teenaged counterparts got a great night of music and dancing.

Meanwhile, back at 1570 on your radio dial, Macy was on the air playing rock n' roll every weekday afternoon and did 4 or 5 hours on the air on Saturdays. And as often as she could be there, Candy was in the control room with Macy. He did all kinds of funny comedy bits on the air, including Candy as the weather girl. Macy used sound effects for such stunts as saying it was time for the weather report from the WONA weather girl and making it sound like she was raising the creaky window and poking her head out.

Then Macy would ask for the weather report, and Candy would announce, "Yep, it's raining," or some other unhelpful information.

Then the day came when Macy graduated from high school and was about to go to college at LSU and to New York to serve as the vice president and later president of a prestigious national youth organization, National Federation of Temple Youth, which he represented around the nation and the world.

But before Macy left his radio show, in typical Macy style, he went out with a flare. He announced that WONA was conducting a contest to see which listeners could come up with the top 10 reasons "to fire" the Top Pop Rock Jock. The grand prize he offered to the winner was a pair of old tennis shoes.

Macy would say years later that Bob's confidence in him made it possible for Macy to "fly."

FLASHBACK: CANDY JUSTICE

I had so much fun being the weather girl for the Top Pop Rock Jock, and I developed a big crush on Macy. I thought I was not being obvious about it, but I found out years later, I had been quite transparent. On the last day of his radio show, Macy bid his loyal listeners goodbye and left the station.

I felt like crying, but I comforted myself by taking home his and my two favorite 45's — "Groovy Kind of Love" by the Mindbenders and "Nowhere Man" by the Beatles. Macy would never know I took them home, I reasoned.

My plan was to play the records over and over and over, something I still do with my favorite music in my iPod. There was just one little hitch in my plan — I left the 45's in my mom's car in the summer heat and they promptly warped beyond playing.

Then to everyone's surprise, Macy came back for one more show and called his weather girl to come join him on the air. As the end of the show loomed, Macy suddenly got the brilliant idea of ending his tenure as the Top Pop Rock Jock by self-effacingly playing the record "Nowhere Man" as his final exit. I wasn't about to admit that I had taken the "Nowhere Man" record so I could use the music to mourn his farewell. So, as he frantically searched for the "Nowhere Man" record, he urged me to help him find it. I disingenuously "searched" for it until he finally had to give up. I didn't confess my sin until 40 years later.

Growing Up in Small Town Mississippi In the 50s and 60s

Several years ago, Bryan was telling a story to his young daughter. She interrupted him and asked, "Daddy, is this another St. Winona story?"

Bryan chuckled and admitted, "Yes, Kristen, I guess it is."

Small Southern towns were magical places in magical times, especially if you were not black and were not poor. Life was somewhat idyllic, at times too sheltered and too isolated from the outside world, but, for many, sublime.

Because there was a friendliness among black and white residents of Winona, it was easy for white people to convince themselves that racial discrimination did not exist. But it did, of course, as it did everywhere.

News and ideas came from local newspapers, local radio stations and from television stations within the state. There were no national newspapers like *USA Today*, and the television networks only provided a nightly, 15-minute news summary each weekday.

This lack of outside influence often gave people a secure sense of isolationism and a feeling they weren't really affected by the outside world. It wasn't until later that the perception changed.

Everyone said, "Yes sir" and "Yes ma'am" to their elders. An 80-year-old man in town said "Yes ma'am" to his 100-year-old aunt. Young people addressed their elders by their last names, Mrs. Jones, or called them "Mr. Joe" or "Miss Bonnie." The same teachers taught the same grade levels and subjects year after year, often schooling several generations of the same family.

Miss Ada Ballard, probably one of the most infamous of these teachers, was the stereotypical "old maid" who never married and devoted her life to her students. She was stern and demanding but loved her students. Miss Ada taught several generations of fifth graders. She also taught many of these students in Sunday School at the Methodist Church, although all her public school students also learned the Ten Commandments, the books of the Bible and recited Bible verses in class during the week.

Young people went to the movies on Saturday night and Sunday afternoons after church. Sundays and Mondays were for Tarzan movies, Elvis musicals and epic blockbusters like *Ben Hur* and *The Ten Commandments*. Tuesdays, Wednesdays and Thursdays featured films for the grown-ups, while Friday and Saturday were reserved for shoot-'em-up Westerns where the heroes wore white hats and only kissed their horses. Admission was 10 cents if you were under 12 and 39 cents if you were older. Popcorn, candy and drinks were just 5 cents each.

Parents would drop their children off for the whole afternoon, armed with 25 cents and ready to sit through a cartoon, coming attractions, a serial and a double feature (two movies for the price of one). Sometimes they sat through all of this a second time without having to pay for another ticket. The boys made fun of the girls when they sobbed as Elvis' character died at the end of *Love Me Tender* and the girls laughed at the boys who sat through Elvis and *Viva Las Vegas* for the second showing just to see Ann-Margret dance again. Forty-five years later, when she was a guest on a TV special Bryan produced, she laughed and told him she was flattered when he told her about those early crushes.

    In the late fifties, even though television was growing in popularity, not everyone had a TV set. Families would sometimes visit neighbors so they could watch their favorite shows, often bringing food over to make it a festive night. Adults and kids sat together in the living room on couches, plush cushions or kitchen chairs or on bed pillows strewn on the floor. On evenings with pleasant weather, people would bring lawn chairs and refreshments downtown to sit in front of the Dacus Furniture Store picture window and watch the conveniently placed black and white TV in the display area. A speaker mounted outside the store brought the sound. After the 10 p.m. news, the owner would go downtown and turn off the television.

    Downtown Winona was compact and always tidy. Almost every store was run by the people who owned it. They worked hard during the week from 7 a.m.-7 p.m., often going home to eat dinner (the biggest meal of the day, usually at noon; supper was the light evening meal). take a nap and walk back to work. On Saturdays the days were longer and the crowds were bigger. You often had to walk in the downtown streets because the sidewalks were overflowing with shoppers from in-town residents to the multitudes who brought their entire families in from the farms to get their weekly groceries, shop for clothes and supplies and maybe see a movie. The stores were open from 7 a.m. until 9 p.m. or later on Saturdays to accommodate the crowds.

Friday nights in the fall were reserved for high school football games. Everyone who wasn't on the team, a cheerleader or in the band packed the wooden bleachers for the 7 o'clock kick-off. Teachers worked the ticket booths and parents and service clubs volunteered to sell hot dogs, popcorn, peanuts and drinks in the concession stands.

After every home game, students, players and band members would walk, drive or hitch a ride to the Community House for the post-game dance. A different homeroom class would be assigned each week to host the party, complete with decorations, cookies and punch. One class member was given a couple of rolls of coins and stood by the jukebox to make sure records played and requests were filled. At 5 cents a play or six plays for a quarter, two rolls easily lasted the night.

The band travelled to out-of-town games as far as 90 miles away in two school buses. On the way home after the game, the buses would stop at a locally owned drive-in (restaurant, not movie) so the students could hurriedly order burgers, fries, milkshakes and drinks from the weary staff that only moments before had been looking forward to closing for the night. However, the owners, who were usually working there themselves, loved the windfall of the unexpected rush of business.

People trusted each other back then. Houses were left unlocked day and night and often even when people went on vacation. Keys were left in the car and nobody took them. Merchants extended credit, usually just by taping a ticket to the wall next to the cash register, waiting to be taken care of on pay day. When Bryan was 10 years old, his uncle regularly sent him through an adjoining alley to the bank to deposit the previous day's grocery store receipts. Bryan clutched the bag full of cash as he walked casually through the streets, safe and unafraid.

One afternoon a week in the summer, the downtown streets were deserted. To make up for their long, six-day week, the merchants closed at noon on Wednesdays to spend time with their families or to find time for their own chores and hobbies. The two drugstores in town took turns staying open so people would have a place to fill emergency prescriptions or to take care of last-minute health needs. McDougall's would stay open Wednesday afternoons, and Moorman's Rexall Pharmacy would open for a few hours on Sunday afternoon. The next week they would reverse the days and times, making sure the residents' needs were always covered.

People didn't know they didn't have cell phones, iPods, calculators or computers. Students learned to do math in their heads, looked up information in the encyclopedia or to find amusement for themselves. Teenagers drove endlessly through and around the town, a 10-minute excursion repeated many times through the evening. People chipped in their dimes and quarters to put a dollar's worth of gas (at 20 cents a gallon) in the car for the evening.

For a big night, friends drove 25 miles north on a two-lane highway to go to a dance in Grenada or travelled an equal distance west to Greenwood to go bowling. People visited with each other, socialized at church or at the country club, cranked homemade ice cream in the summer, shelled peas and pecans, snapped beans, picked blackberries, made jelly, or canned fruits and vegetables to be eaten in the winter.

Nicknames abounded. Boy, did they abound. Some nicknames were so much a part of a person that many people didn't know their real names. Most people had no remembrance that Monkey was really Larry Grantham. Just ask Goose Lowery, Goat Cooke or Turkey Lamb. Goddoggit Herring was once the local sheriff and folks he arrested might have faced Judge Soggy Sweat in court. If they were in real trouble, Rev. Tomato Tillman would pray for their souls.

Nicknames even spread across generations. You had to be specific so people would understand you were talking about Big Foots and not Little Foots Evans. Little Chicken was Big Chicken Crenshaw's oldest son. Likewise for Big Skeeter and Little Skeeter or Big Zook and Little Zook (not to be confused with his baby brother Chew). Bryan's mother, Bibby, was the youngest of seven children. He grew up with Aunt Big, Aunt Little, Uncle Son, Uncle Bud, Big Joe and Aunt Majie. He didn't know their real names for years.

Summers offered new outlets for youthful adventures. Little League baseball filled the season with daytime practices and night games. Every boy remembers his first glove, his first real cleats and his first uniform. Teams from the town and teams from as far as 10 miles away played hard-fought games and then went together to the Satellite Drive-in for a burger and coke or to the Mug and Cone for a root beer float. The swimming pool (whites only) opened right after school was out for the summer. An inexpensive pass allowed unlimited access to the pool in both the daylight and evening sessions for the entire summer.

Coaches found summer work running the pool, while older students manned the towers as lifeguards or worked in the concession stands. Kids couldn't figure out why they had to take a shower *before* getting in the pool. The rule robbed them of the refreshing thrill of your hot body cooling off when you jumped in the cold pool water.

Before McDonald's, Wendy's or Burger King, there were locally owned drive-in restaurants (not to be confused with drive-in theaters where you could get in for 25 cents a person, not counting the people hidden in the trunk).

The Satellite Drive-in was the center of the collective teen universe. Before, during or after the movies, parties, church, cruising, dates, ball games or doing nothing, everyone went to the Satellite where Cokes and fries were 10 cents and a fully loaded hamburger was 15 cents. Milkshakes were real and made on the spot. Just the sound of a chocolate, vanilla or strawberry shake swirling behind the counter made your mouth water. Kids in cars cruised through the parking lot looking for friends to hook up with or pulled into one of the slots where you could place your order and have it brought to the car.

Spacious tables inside invited people to crowd around to share laughs, miseries, stories and food. Romances budded and fell by the wayside. Manager Ken West extended credit when folks were broke and introduced patrons to French fries and gravy. Life was good. Who had time to be bored?

The American Legion constructed a man-made lake on the outskirts of town. Legion Lake offered a free place to swim, fish, boat and water ski (on a limited scale). The yearly fishing rodeo was popular with youngsters, and families flocked to the annual American Legion Fish Fry to enjoy their fill of fish, hushpuppies and homemade slaw.

The biggest draw at Legion Lake, though, was the skating rink, a large building with a wooden floor located next to the lake. It was filled on the weekend as people skated alone, together in couples or in large groups. Rock and roll music competed with the reverberations of hundreds of skate wheels pounding the floor and the shouts and squeals of young people, teenagers and a few brave adults circling the arena.

The loudspeaker sometimes announced special events such as races, girls only or the more raucous boys only portion. The favorite announcement, however, was for "couples only," the chance to skate with a special someone or to make a cool move on a potential special someone. Or to completely screw up a cool move on a potential special someone. It was a warm summer evening and Bryan had been carefully planning his move for at least an hour. Then the moment came. He knew the next song was going to be a couples only ballad, so he carefully positioned himself right behind Pamela Sue Mortimer.

As the previous record ended and "Couples Only" was announced, Bryan artfully skated up to Pamela Sue, smoothly took her hand, gallantly put his arm around her waist…and kicked her skates out from under her. As she thudded to the floor, Bryan caught his balance and stayed on his feet. For some reason she never went out with him.

Youthful social life centered around the churches. Teens flocked to Sunday school and church on Sundays and sometimes on Sunday night and Wednesday night, as well as formal and informal activities throughout the year. The larger Baptist Church had a full time youth director and the Methodist Church hired a college student every summer to be the youth leader. It didn't matter what church you attended. The activities were open to everyone as clusters of friends moved from one church and one activity to another. Most of the church-sponsored activities didn't have an overt religious theme or lesson. Instead, the churches and the leaders concentrated on making sure young people had safe places to gather for fun and productive things to do. Religion came on Sunday.

Progressive suppers were a big event, filling an entire evening with food and games. The idea was simple. A group started out the evening by having an appetizer at someone's house and usually playing a game or singing around a piano. A walk (hardly ever a car ride) to another home provided the first entrée of the evening and more games. As the evening progressed, so did the supper. By the end of the night, everyone had consumed a full meal and had enjoyed a variety of games, music and dancing. Parents enjoyed the evening because they knew where the kids were. Teens had fun because they were with their friends.

Scavenger hunts were always popular. After dividing into teams, each team would get an identical list of obscure items to gather from around town. The team that got the most items on the list in the time limit (usually a couple of hours) was the winner. The prizes didn't matter. What counted was being on the winning team. Armed with their lists, they would set out into the night and go door to door asking the almost always amused residents if they had such items as a stick of gum, a plastic fork, an empty plastic bag, a copy of the *Winona Times* from three weeks ago or a small bag of used coffee grounds.

There was always at least one item that was much harder to find. The key to winning often depended on which team managed to find that obscure item and get back to the church the fastest. One night, Bryan and his teammates discovered something on the list that they quickly realized could be their key to victory – Bob Chisholm's signature.

Not only did Bryan have an inside track with Bob, he also had his $6 WONA paycheck in his pocket, with Bob's signature. Bob had one of the worst signatures anyone ever tried to read. It started with a scribble that could only generously be described as a B and was followed by a scrawled single line that looked like a drunken snake.

As soon as Bryan saw the list he ran to the phone and called Bob. After telling him about the now-coveted signature (Bob knew nothing about it), Bryan asked him not to answer the door if anyone came by and rang the doorbell. Bob agreed to join the conspiracy, promising to stay out of the living room and to turn off the porch light to discourage visitors. For the next two hours, teams fruitlessly rang Bob's doorbell, only to be thwarted by the unanswered door. Bryan's team, of course, won the night by combining his paycheck with a little bit of larceny.

Parents didn't worry where teenagers were after dark. They knew their kids were with their friends and that they were safe. If that sounds naïve, it wasn't. The fact was, young people in the town had 3,000 parents. If anyone got into any mischief or even looked like they might, a nearby adult was sure to ask, "Do you think your momma would want you to do that?" If someone happened to be at a friend's house around supper time, they were automatically invited to stay and eat.

Looking back, however, there was one type of recreation that only seemed like a good idea at the time. In the fifties and sixties, the chemical DDT was sprayed extensively to kill bugs on crops or to kill mosquitoes in town. All summer long, a truck drove through the streets, dispensing a thick fog of DDT in every neighborhood. Hordes of kids gleefully ran behind the truck, often completely hidden as they darted in and out of the oily, smelly mist. It's amazing now that people thought this was fun, or that parents thought nothing of their kids' pastime. That was before the government banned the use of DDT because it was found to cause cancer. Kids didn't know that back then. Parents didn't know. Nobody knew. Only scientist

Rachel Carson seemed to know how deadly DDT was and she told the world with her controversial book *Silent Spring*.

The Fairgrounds on the outskirts of town provided plenty of family entertainment. The Montgomery County Fair drew people not only from Winona, but also from Vaiden, Carrollton, Blackhawk, Kilmichael, Sweatman, Lodi, Stewart (pronounced "Stirt") and Poplar Creek. Competition to recognize the best preserves, canned goods, cakes, pies, and homemade quilts in the county drew scores of entrants. Cattle, horses, sheep, goats and assorted small animals competed for blue ribbons. Young FFA, FHA, and 4-H Club members were judged on their expertise in year-long projects.

Dance contests filled time as judges decided who would be crowned as "Fairest of the Fair." Sometimes, a small rodeo came to town, featuring bucking horses, bull riders, calf ropers, barrel racers and the ever-present clowns with their corny jokes and fearlessness keeping enraged bulls away from their erstwhile riders. Carnivals brought sideshows, barkers, games of chance and skill and rides that turned, twirled and circled, oblivious to the fact someone might actually throw up on Nina Gail Ingram on the Tilt-A-Whirl in mid-whirl. In Bryan's defense, he had always had an issue with motion sickness.

Adults had their own entertainment. Movies, football and basketball games, softball and little league contests were always available. Bridge clubs, weekly supper clubs, book clubs and canasta or Rook gatherings often took the place of television. The country club offered tennis, fishing, swimming and golf, as well as the occasional dance. The grown-ups even had access, sort of, to adult beverages. Drinking them was not against the law. Buying them, however, was. Mississippi was the last state in the country to

Checkers was a favorite pastime in and around Winona in the 1970s. In this photo, taken not far from Winona, a blacksmith, right, and his friend play a game during a lull in the horseshoeing business. Photo by James L. Dickerson /Greenwood Commonwealth.

outlaw the sale or purchase of alcoholic beverages or transporting them across the state line.

An amendment to the law did allow for what was called "local option." Individual counties could vote to allow the sale of beer if a majority of voters were in favor of it. This was not an easy proposition. Because the churches fought so hard against this option, citing the evils of "whiskey," (any **alcohol-based beverage was universally described as "whiskey" by those opposing it**) most congregation members, in the local parlance, staggered to the polls and voted dry.

Winona was the county seat of a very dry Montgomery County. Fortunately, if you were so inclined, neighboring Carroll County allowed the sale of beer. Every night, especially Friday and Saturday nights, people drove to the "county line" to enjoy dinner and a beverage or six at Chamblees or the Ole Rebel. While the fare at these establishments could not be described as haute cuisine, they served a purpose and they were popular.

As tranquil as that time seemed, there was also a dark cloud that hovered over the South. The price for isolation was a much narrower view of the world. In the fifties and sixties, the role of women was much too easily defined. Although there were no laws to mandate it, the primary responsibility of a woman was to take care of the house and support her husband's work and hobbies.

Women went to college to find a suitable husband, her MRS degree. If a woman worked outside the house, she was generally limited to being a secretary, nurse, teacher or factory worker. The idea of a female being a doctor, lawyer or pilot wasn't even given a thought.

If she did work an outside job, a woman was still expected to be home in time to cook and serve dinner, clean the house, take care of the kids and do the laundry. Women folk were patronized not to "worry their pretty little heads" about matters. That was a man's job. Wow. While it may be embarrassing to think about that now, that is the way it was back then.

Years later, younger friends sometimes asked Candy how gender discrimination of the 1950s, 60s and 70s had affected her career and personal life. Those younger women were surprised, even shocked, by Candy's answer: "If sexism and feminism existed when I was in high school, college and in my first job as a newspaper reporter, I didn't know it and neither did my mother, who had her own daily award-winning radio show on WONA and was an independent woman who made her own decisions on everything."

As Candy became a young adult, she overheard a few men making degrading sexual remarks about her sometimes, but she chose to ignore them and felt secure in who she was. As she later recalled:

> I never felt discriminated against because of my gender in any appreciable way whether as a child, teenager, wife, mother, single or divorced woman or more recently as a widow. Certainly, I never felt discriminated against when I was a newspaper reporter and later a local and national magazine writer. The only serious discrimination I have felt in my entire life has been in recent years when it was clear to me that some, *but not most,* of my younger University colleagues saw me as too old to deserve respect. The *least* discrimination I ever experienced was while working as a journalist. No editor ever said of me, 'Don't send Candy to cover that — it's dark outside and in a dangerous neighborhood.' My editors at the *Press-Scimitar,* where I worked as a reporter covering news for 10 years, treated me exactly as they treated my male colleagues. I would have been furious if they had treated me better or worse than the men, but that was not the case. I was either fortunate or oblivious.

Granted, Candy was white, middle class, well-educated and raised in a first-world country by parents who taught her to be independent, all of which put her in a privileged class from most women in the world.

"I knew that sexism and gender discrimination do very much exist in this country," Candy said, "but I have to say truthfully that I don't feel my being a woman has ever been a major disadvantage for me personally. However, I would never in any way speak for other women."

However, when Candy was a young reporter at the *Press-Scimitar,* she did have one experience that she found to be misguided at best and insulting at worst. Her fellow female journalists and dear friends Peggy Burch, Deborah DeBois and she were among those who received invitations from the Chamber of Commerce to a citywide luncheon called "Salute to Women Who Work." All three of them were outraged that somebody thought that women who had paying jobs were so unusual and so laudable that they should be patted on the back by men. So they did not accept the invitations and just went about their usual self-sufficient ways.

••••••••••

Racial discrimination, however, among women and men in all aspects of society, was more insidious. Though segregation was an accepted fact by whites and even some Black people in the years before 1960, the rumblings of change were rising in the early 1960s. Small towns operated two schools – White and Colored (when people were being polite).

The "separate but equal" status mandated by the Supreme Court in the historic 1896 *Plessey v Ferguson* decision was equal in name only. Funding, facilities, faculties, supplies and equipment in the non-white schools were almost always inferior. The 1954 *Brown v Topeka, Kansas Board of Education* ruling had ordered schools to desegregate with "all deliberate speed." Large and small southern cities had a much broader definition of that term than the Court envisioned. Things were fine the way they were, many white people reasoned.

Restroom and water fountains were clearly delineated as being exclusively for *White* or *Colored.* The Trailways bus station had separate waiting areas and separate seating on the bus. No one of either race at first dared challenge this practice. Restaurants only served white patrons, unless "coloreds" got a table in the kitchen. Black people could get into the movie theater, but they had to come in through the side entrance and could only sit in the balcony. If they wanted refreshments, they had to buy their food and drinks through a tiny window at the back of the concession stand. Even the funeral homes and cemeteries kept the races apart after they were dead.

Groups were formed to unofficially enforce and promote these standards. The Ku Klux Klan and the White Citizens Council openly reminded people that whites were superior to Blacks and that Jews and Catholics presented a threat to "real" Americans. Mississippi television stations aired a (free) weekly program, *Citizen's Council Forum"* dedicated to, "The preservation of states' rights and racial integrity." As with other southern radio stations, WONA programming was mainly aimed at the white audience. For instance, the station reported notices from white funeral homes, but not the black funeral home.

Bryan did a five-minute high school news program three afternoons a week, but the "colored" school had no such program. At that time, in spite of the 1954 Supreme Court decision forbidding separate school systems, the city had different schools for Black students and white students.

The official name for the school system was "The Winona Separate School District." Bob recognized all these inequities and was slowly able to introduce changes to combat them. He started with the Negro Activity Calendar, a five-minute weekly program prepared and hosted by African Americans and dedicated to publicizing events and news of interest to the Negro community. At that time, "negro" and "colored" were considered the respectful terms for who would later be called "Black people" and even later "African Americans."

WONA started airing funeral notices from the Black funeral home as part of its morning coverage. The station even included interviews with the J.J. Knox football coach during football season. There was some opposition, but Bob never yielded to such pressure. Public attitudes were slowly beginning to change, although grudgingly at times. To the credit of the city and the people, attitudes began to change in the sixties. Bob Chisholm and WONA were an integral part of this transformation.

**Fannie Lou Hamer at the Democratic Convention
Library of Congress**

Chapter 5

"I'm sick and tired of being sick and tired."
— Fannie Lou Hamer

When Fannie Lou Hamer was a little girl — the youngest of 20 children of sharecroppers on a Mississippi plantation — she single-handedly picked 200-300 pounds of cotton a day, despite her limp from untreated polio.

There wasn't much food for the family and sometimes they had to wrap their feet in rags for lack of shoes. Still, the family was able to save up enough money to rent some land and buy a tractor, only to have a white neighbor poison their cattle, leaving them financially worse off than they had been to begin with.

Young Fannie Lou, exhausted and discouraged, told her mother that things had gotten so bad that she was starting to wish she was white. But her mother was quick to set her straight, though not unkindly.

"Don't ever, ever say that," Mrs. Ella Townsend said to her youngest daughter. "You respect yourself as a little black child, and as you grow older, respect yourself as a Black woman. Then one day, other people will respect you."

Mrs. Townsend was right — Fannie Lou Hamer went on eventually to be a famous and respected civic rights and women's rights activist. And she was always an advocate for poor people of all races. When she died in 1977 at the age of 59, U.S. Ambassador to the United Nations Andrew Young gave the eulogy in Ruleville, Mississippi, and over 1,500 people attended the memorial service. A high school in the Bronx, a borough of New York City, was named Fannie Lou Hamer Freedom High School, one of many tributes to her after her death.

But in between, Mrs. Hamer's life was extremely eventful — sometimes rewarding and triumphant and other times brutal and unfair. Her detractors often cast doubt on her message by calling her illiterate, ignorant and worse, but though she had to drop out of school in 6th grade, she was none of those things. She loved to read and taught others to read and write, memorized and recited poetry and she won spelling bees. She was beautifully eloquent and smart in the eyes of those who could put their prejudices aside long enough to see and hear the truth.

Mrs. Hamer was born in Montgomery County, Mississippi, and her parents, Mr. and Mrs. James Lee Townsend, lived on Highway 82, east of Winona. When Fannie Lou was two years old, her family moved to Sunflower County, Mississippi, to work as sharecroppers on Marlow Plantation near Ruleville. Her father was also a Baptist minister.

When Fannie Lou Townsend married Perry "Pap" Hamer from Kilmichael, Mississippi, who drove a tractor on the Marlow plantation, they were looking forward to starting a family, but when Mrs. Hamer went into the hospital to have minor surgery to remove a tumor, the white doctor also performed a hysterectomy on her, without her permission.

Forced sterilization was a common method used at that time to prevent poor, Black and Native American women from having children. Many in the Black community referred to those operations as a "Mississippi appendectomy." The Hamers adopted two daughters.

In the early 1960s, Mrs. Hamer became interested in registering to vote. She was denied that right on her first two tries, and her boss on the plantation fired her for trying to register and told her to leave his land. The Hamer family moved between the homes of friends for several days until Mrs. Hamer was shot at 15 times, which caused the family to flee to Tallahatchie County for three months, fearing retaliation by the Ku Klux Klan in Sunflower County.

Looking back on that, Mrs. Hamer was quoted as saying, "I guess if I'd had any sense, I'd have been a little scared, but what was the point of being scared? The only thing they could do was kill me, and it kinda seemed like they'd been trying to do that a little bit at a time since I could remember."

After becoming a field secretary for the Student Nonviolent Coordinating Committee in 1963, Mrs. Hamer went to a voter registration workshop in South Carolina. On the trip home, the Continental Trailways bus carrying her and five other activists (Annell Ponder, Euvester Simpson, Rosemary Freeman, James West and teenager June Johnson) made a rest stop at the bus station on Highway 51 in Winona, Mississippi.

Mrs. Hamer stayed on the bus, but the other five went inside the bus terminal and sat down at the lunch counter. The white waitress working there refused to serve them, and a Highway Patrolman ordered them to leave.

Ponder reminded the patrolman that the Supreme Court had ruled that segregated rest stops were illegal. Mrs. Hamer got off the bus to see what was going on, and when she tried to get back on the bus, she was arrested.

Once they were booked at the Winona jail, Mrs. Hamer said she heard "horrible screams" from other cells where her fellow activists were being held. She said the law enforcement officers were calling the activists "nigger" and using violence and torture to try to force them to say "Yes, sir" to the law officers.

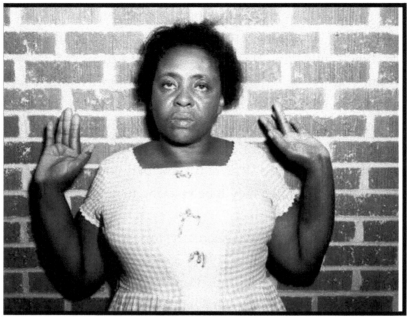
Fannie Lou Hamer at the Winona jail   FBI Photo

Then three white men came to Mrs. Hamer's cell, and one told her, "We are going to make you wish you was dead." The men forced her to lie face down in the cell bunk and ordered two black male prisoners to beat her with a club.

They hit her in the back over and over, causing permanent kidney damage, and hit her in the head, causing her to have a blood clot behind her eye and lose partial sight in one eye. The men also sexually molested her.

Mrs. Hamer's description of the beating ended with her later saying, "I was in jail when Medgar Evers (activist and decorated World War II veteran) was murdered (in his driveway in Jackson, Mississippi.)

When Manager of WONA Bob Chisholm, heard that Civil Rights activists, including Fannie Lou Hamer, were being held at the Winona jail, he went over there and saw that the activists' names were on the arrest log, and he said the arresting officers seemed very proud of themselves. Bob had to go do something back at the radio station but told them he was coming back soon to get information for the news story that would air on the radio news the next morning.

Bob always regretted leaving the jail, because when he returned, the arrest log was completely blank. Bob asked for the sheet that had the activists' names on it and the arrest report telling what happened at the bus station.

The arresting officers said he must be imagining things, that they had not arrested anybody, and they had never told him Hamer and the others had been arrested. Of course, he knew they were lying and told them so, but they stuck to their lie. He learned from that experience never to tell the Winona police that he was coming back for information. Nonetheless, the story was on Chisholm's WONA newscast the next morning with the limited details he had.

FLASHBACK: BRYAN COTTINGHAM

Byron de la Beckwith was a white supremacist accused of ambushing and killing Medgar Evers on June 12, 1963. His first two trials ended with a hung jury. In 1994, new evidence was found, and the case was re-opened. Beckwith was found guilty and, at the age of 71, was sentenced to life in prison. He died there seven years later.

I encountered Beckwith shortly after his second mistrial. He had come to Winona at the invitation of several businessmen who brought him to WONA to have him interviewed. Bob refused. He didn't want to glorify a man who, by all accounts, had murdered a civil rights activist.

I was in the room with Beckwith and the businessmen as they waited for Bob. The men were smiling and joking with the accused assassin. Finally, one of them poked Beckwith and said with a conspiratorial smile, "Come on, did you really shoot him?"

Beckwith grinned and said, "Well, nigger's dead, ain't he?"

To this day, a chill runs down my back when I think about that moment.

•••••••••

Fannie Lou Hamer, LBJ's Worst Nightmare

Lyndon B. Johnson, who became U.S. president when President John F. Kennedy was assassinated in 1963, is credited with signing the Civil Rights Act of 1964; the Voting Rights Act of 1965; appointing the first Black Supreme Court Justice Thurgood Marshall and championing such progressive reforms as Medicare, Head Start and the War on Poverty.

He was also the person who did everything in his power to try to bring down Civil Rights activist Fannie Lou Hamer, which leaves one to question if some of his progressive achievements were more motivated by political gain than "doing the right thing."

When John F. Kennedy was running for president in 1960, LBJ, a rough-around-the-edges Texan, was chosen as JFK's running mate partially because he was thought to be someone who would be able to win over Southern Democratic voters, who might disapprove of Kennedy, a Catholic and wealthy New England elite.

JFK and LBJ were not known to like each other, to put it mildly. Johnson, who had had a very successful 24 years in Congress and the U.S. Senate, resented playing second fiddle to a young rich boy like Kennedy, who had graduated from Harvard and had just been a senator for seven years. The Kennedy clan looked down on Johnson, whom they considered crude, poorly educated and unsophisticated.

The Kennedy/Johnson ticket was widely regarded in political circles as a marriage of convenience.

Fannie Lou Hamer and President Lyndon Johnson crossed paths politically in 1964. Perhaps "butted heads" says it better. Mrs. Hamer's mother had taught her to "stand up no matter what the odds." Mrs. Hamer and her supporters had traveled to Atlantic City to try to convince the Democratic National Committee's credentials committee to seat Mrs. Hamer's Mississippi Freedom Democratic Party delegation, an integrated coalition of delegates, instead of the all-white Democratic delegation from Mississippi — a delegation dominated by segregationist politicians.

Johnson, who knew he probably could not get re-elected without Southern Democrats' votes, was livid over Mrs. Hamer's efforts. He told his political advisers to find a way to stop Fannie Lou Hamer and her party. When the advisers tried to pressure her into dropping her appeal to the credentials committee, Mrs. Hamer refused. LBJ sent Hubert Humphrey with orders to solve "the Mississippi problem."

Humphrey told Mrs. Hamer that Johnson was offering a compromise of two at-large delegates from her party with the proviso that Fannie Lou Hamer could not be one of them. Humphrey said to her, "The President has said he will not let that illiterate woman speak on the floor of the Democratic convention," and that Humphrey's bid to be the vice-presidential candidate hinged on Hamer's party accepting the compromise.

"I was amazed," Mrs. Hamer said years later, "and I said, 'Well, Mr. Humphrey, do you mean to tell me that your position is more important to you than 400,000 Black people's lives?"

The Mississippi Freedom Democratic Party voted to reject the compromise. And Fannie Lou Hamer did indeed speak on the floor

**President Lyndon Johnson signs Civil Rights Act of 1968.
Photo by Warren K. Leffler, Library of Congress.**

of the convention. Dressed in a summer print dress with a white pocketbook on her arm, pushing her way through the crowd of men, she spoke for 13 electrifying minutes with no notes. She told about being fired from her job when she tried to register to vote, about gunshots from the Ku Klux Klan and she described in detail her brutal beating in the Winona, Mississippi, jail. Then she picked up her purse and left the convention hall with her full dignity intact.

When she and her supporters got back to their hotel, they found out that LBJ had called an unplanned press conference to keep her speech from getting on TV. But Mrs. Hamer got the last word — her speech was so moving that the national networks ran it on TV anyhow for the whole country to see. And that improvised speech has been counted by many to be one of the greatest of the Civil Rights Era.

∙∙∙∙∙∙∙∙∙∙∙

On June 9, 2022, a historical marker was erected in a ceremony at the site of the old jail in Winona at the corner of Sterling and Jones Streets, exactly 59 years after Fannie Lou Hamer's near fatal beating by police there.

**Winona Post Office, gateway to the outside world.
Photo courtesy Bain Hughes.**

Chapter 6

The Bad Guys Almost Win

Everybody listened to WONA, including Bob Chisholm's enemies — *especially* Bob's enemies.

A courageous reporter makes a lot of enemies along the way — people who prefer that their actions stay secret and get angry when light is shined on what they say or do. Some of their actions are illegal, while most are simply unethical or self-serving. Publicly known truth about those actions or attitudes sometimes makes it hard for them to maintain their reputations as upstanding citizens or as public officials who should be re-elected.

During Bob Chisholm's years as a newsman (he never called himself a reporter), he faced all kinds of obstacles including being beat up, attempts to get him fired, government meetings held in secret so he could not attend and report on them and businesses discontinuing their advertising to punish him and the radio station.

Many of those attempts at intimidation back-fired because in a small town everybody knows everybody and word gets out about the misdeeds. The good people of Winona — and most Winonians were and are good people — would phone the perpetrators or stop them on the street and give them a piece of their minds. Often, they would have heard about the wrong-doing of public officials on Chisholm's 7 a.m. morning news on WONA.

Bob survived all those assaults — but the one attack that came perilously close to bringing him and WONA down was in the form of a complaint to the Federal Communications Commission (FCC) in 1964. The headline on page one of the Winona Times was: *WONA*

World vs. Bob Chisholm

charged with promoting discord, hatred.

The newspaper story began this way:

A petition charging local radio station WONA with "distortions, prejudices and a slanted point of view calculated to produce discord, hatred and strife" has been filed with the Federal Communications Commission in Washington.

The five-page complaint, signed by 18 officials and ex-officials of the city and county governments, alleged that "it would be to the best interest of the people of the community if WONA's license to operate was revoked by the government."

The Winona Times story went on to quote the complaint to the FCC this way:

"The petition cites several instances in which the station's news commentator Bob Chisholm is purported to have deliberately misquoted or implied untrue facts concerning local happenings and citizens involved. Investigation of the daily newscast at 7 a.m. will reveal, periodically and systematically, distortions and slanted news. This is a community problem."

If that complaint had been filed today, it would be easy for the FCC investigators in Washington, D.C., to find the daily newscasts online and decide for themselves if the accusations were warranted, but this was 1964. Probably those filing the complaint were aware that they could make this suggestion without fear of the FCC actually being able to follow through on listening to the WONA morning news.

The *Winona Times* story goes on: "Chisholm, station manager and secretary-treasurer of the corporation owning the station, said in a statement, the station 'categorically denies all allegations made and implied in the complaint.'"

"Chisholm noted that a reply to the charges is being prepared for the FCC (by a Washington, D.C., communications attorney hired by WONA). 'We believe that our answer will show beyond a shadow of a doubt that all charges are baseless,'" Chisholm declared in the statement.

Chisholm said the station has received "overwhelming expressions of shock and amazement from the public" concerning the charges.

"We do not have to prove the caliber of our activities to the people of this area," Chisholm is quoted as saying in the *Winona Times* article. "However, the officials of the FCC are not within our listening area, and we must prepare and present to them sufficient evidence upon which they can make an intelligent judgment of this very serious matter."

Chisholm said that "despite the expense and inconvenience involved, we are most appreciative of this opportunity to present the facts to the FCC and to answer the complaint fully and factually."

The Winona Times article ended with the names of the men listed by the FCC as requesting the investigation and revocation of license: Rupert Ringold, M.C. Billingsley, Davis Hurt, Jack Groce, V.C. Vance, T.J. Herod, E.W. Patridge, Clarence Oliver, R.L. Varner, Bill Surrell, A.A. Stidham, Dillard Biggers, Marion Williams, W.F. Jefcoat, Roy Thompson, Marvin Able, Albert Hayward and J.W. Braswell.

On the list of those who had filed the FCC complaint, many of them had been angry with Bob for years for his truthful reporting, a few going so far as to make death threats against Chisholm. When Candy was a child, she answered her family's home phone one night and the caller said, "We're going to kill your daddy." That caller was one of the local men who was among those filing the complaint with the FCC.

How could the FCC have life and death Control over Winona's radio station?

Unlike newspapers, which under the U.S. Constitution have complete First Amendment rights and protections — when radio came along, Congress saw fit to regulate it.

The reasoning given was that theoretically anyone could establish their own newspaper, but the number of radio stations was limited by the scarcity of frequencies.

Therefore, people cannot start their own radio stations without applying to the FCC for a license and being assigned a frequency, and the FCC has the authority to revoke that license.

The FCC was created in 1934 and was made up of a 7-person board meant to operate as an independent regulatory government agency. But almost from the beginning, the FCC was *not* independent because the board members were appointed by the President of the United States and were subject to Congressional approval. The FCC's enormous power has always been susceptible to political influence and interference by whichever political party was in power.

The 1960s was a decade that saw much weaponizing of the FCC's power. A number of radio and television stations lost their licenses because the FCC ruled their programming was not acceptable.

The FCC's Fairness Doctrine was especially perilous for broadcasters wishing to hold on to their licenses because it required that broadcasters both cover controversial topics of public importance *and* reflect differing viewpoints in a fair manner. But, of course, on a daily basis, who determines what is fair — a very subjective concept. The Fairness Doctrine's eventual abolishment in 1987 was partially connected to credible claims that broadcast stations should be granted the same First Amendment protections that newspapers and magazines had enjoyed since the establishment of the nation. But that was no help to WONA in 1964.

Fighting Back

Chisholm had always fought his own battles with truth and public support, but with the all-powerful FCC holding an axe over WONA's neck, station manager Bob Chisholm and station owner Bob Evans, Sr. realized they needed big-time professional help. Enter Gene Bechtel, a highly respected communications attorney, who was a partner in a Washington, D. C., law firm.

Chisholm and Bechtel began feverishly putting together WONA's formal response to the FCC complaint, sometimes working in Winona and sometimes in Washington. They only had three months to gather evidence and write the response. Meanwhile, Chisholm continued to work 15 hours a day, seven days a week at the station, as he always had.

There was one almost insurmountable problem — this was the 1960s, a period in FCC history where broadcasters, especially in Southern states, were assumed guilty unless they could prove themselves innocent.

During that decade, the U.S. Court of Appeals in an opinion written by Warren Burger, who would later become Chief Justice of the Supreme Court, ordered the FCC to revoke the license of Jackson, Mississippi, television station WLBT, because
of the station's segregationist politics and censorship of NBC News' coverage of the Civil Rights Movement.

So it was an uphill battle for WONA to not be assumed to be racist by the FCC simply because the station was in Mississippi.

Those were terrifying days for Bob and Carol Chisholm, Gene Bechtel and even Candy, who all feared they were about to lose this fight to retain the station's broadcast license.

Then something happened that was very much like the ending of the Jimmy Stewart Christmas movie, "It's a Wonderful Life." And Bob Chisholm was the Jimmy Stewart character — a good man at his wit's end, about to lose everything, thanks to the evil banker Mr. Potter. Although Chisholm wasn't going to kill himself as the Jimmy Stewart character was contemplating, Bob was in the darkest hour of his life and had run out of ideas to save the radio station's license.

FLASHBACK: CANDY JUSTICE

Then a miracle occurred. The wonderful people of Winona, Mississippi, rallied to the rescue of WONA and my parents. The people of Winona, hundreds of them, started writing letters to the FCC describing what the station and Bob and Carol Chisholm meant to the town, explaining that those who had filed the FCC complaint had lied and totally misrepresented the situation to the FCC. The good citizens of Winona began signing petitions to save the station and rescue my parents.

I will always remember my mom and dad's faces as they realized that the radio station was going to be saved by the people of our town. Word had come through Gene Bechtel in Washington that the FCC was so impressed by the grassroots support by Black and white citizens for WONA and Bob Chisholm that the FCC was dismissing the complaint filed by the 18 city and county officials and former officials. As it turned out, regular folks really could successfully fight City Hall.

Like Clarence, the angel in *It's a Wonderful Life*, wrote, "Remember, no man is a failure who has friends."

Martin Luther King and Joan Baez on the 1966 march from Memphis to Jackson, this photo possibly taken in Winona. Photo courtesy Bob Fitch Photography Archive, Department of Special Collections, Stanford University Library.

Chapter 7

Dr. Martin Luther King Comes to Winona

When it became evident that Dr. Martin Luther King, Stokely Carmichael and other Civil Rights leaders would be marching into Winona during the summer of 1966, leaders from the Black and white communities were worried about the safety of the marchers.

Sheriff E.W. "Pop" Wages; Bob Chisholm; Winona Times editor Hembree Brandon; African American educator Dr. Arthur Norwood and Dr. Tom Dulin, superintendent of Winona schools, among other people, began talking among themselves about how they could prevent violence directed at the marchers.

They had good reason to worry. After all, this 220-mile March Against Fear, which had begun in Memphis and was led by James Meredith, the first Black student to attend the University of Mississippi, had already been disrupted by violence. On the second day of Meredith's march, intended to register Black voters in towns between Memphis and Jackson, Mississippi, he was shot by a white sniper Aubrey James Novell, who later pleaded guilty to the crime. Meredith suffered several gunshot wounds and was rushed to a hospital and eventually recovered.

Meredith was no stranger to violence — his registration at Ole Miss on October 1, 1962, accompanied by 127 U.S. Marshals and many other law enforcement officers and National Guardsmen, was followed by a riot that resulted in two civilian deaths.

Three years before the March Against Fear, NAACP field secretary Medgar Evers, 37, who had fought on the beaches of

**James Meredith at Ole Miss graduation ceremony.
Courtesy Special Collections, University of Memphis Library.**

Normandy during World War II, was gunned down in his own driveway in Jackson, Mississippi, by white supremacist Byron De La Beckwith, as Evers' wife and three children waited anxiously inside for him to come home. Evers died at a whites-only hospital, which initially refused to treat him.

When James Meredith was shot on the second day of his voter registration march, King and Carmichael decided to carry on in Meredith's absence, though Meredith recovered enough to rejoin the march when it finished in Jackson later in the summer.

So Winona Sheriff Wages and others had good reason to worry what might happen when the famous civil rights leaders marched into Winona. The Ku Klux Klan was a pretty rag-tag group in Winona by that time, but it only takes one person with a rifle to kill somebody.

Sheriff Wages knew that he didn't have anywhere near the manpower needed to protect King, Carmichael and the other marchers, so the sheriff told Chisholm he was going to try to pre-empt a possible assassination. Someone tipped Pop Wages to the fact that the local Klan was planning to meet in a house out from town several days before the March Against Fear was scheduled to reach Winona.

After everyone was inside the Klan meeting that night, the sheriff quietly arrived and wrote down the license plate numbers of all the cars and then left. The next day, he began paying visits to all the Klansmen at their work places, letting them know in no uncertain terms that if anything — and he meant *anything* — happened to try to hurt or intimidate the famous civil rights leaders or any of the local Black citizens who would march with them and line up to register to vote, the sheriff would be coming after the Klan and they would be very sorry.

Sheriff Wages — who often dropped in at Bob and Carol's house because he and Bob were close friends — took great delight in describing to Bob the looks on the faces of the Klansmen when he told them they would be sorry. He said, in his experience, potential criminals were far more frightened by menacing general threats than by specifics. Bob and Pop Wages got a good ole laugh out of that. Still, they both felt anxiety about what might happen the next day.

Chisholm always went to work about 3:30 or 4 a.m. to prepare for his 7 a.m. newscast, but that day he came back home after the news was over. He told his wife and daughter that he thought it was fine for them to watch the marchers from their front yard on Webster Street, which had a clear view of Summit Street, which the marchers would use to get to the courthouse. But despite the sheriff's best efforts to keep the Klan at bay, Bob told his family he feared the Klan might still do something violent at the courthouse, so he wanted Carol and Candy to stay away from there.

When the marchers left Highway 51 to march down Summit, Carol and Candy were out in front of their house, along with some other neighbors and watched the marchers pass. A young African American woman who worked for the Hightower family, was standing with the rest of the neighbors and as the marchers passed, one of them shouted to her, "Come on, Sister, join us!" Poor Urgie, who was sweet and very shy, was so embarrassed by the marcher's attention that she started to cry and turned her head away. The neighborhood kids and Carol Chisholm comforted Urgie, though the kids did not understand why she was crying.

The Townsend family lived across the street from the Chisholms, and they had a long-time domestic employee and lifelong family friend, Millie Mae Moore, who is African American.

Betty and B.F. Townsend encouraged Miss Moore to go downtown and listen to Dr. King's speech on the steps of the courthouse. At first Miss Moore said she did not want to go, but the Townsends finally talked her into taking advantage of that historical opportunity, and B.F. drove her to the courthouse.

After the marchers disappeared from view as they walked past Lee Funeral Home on the corner, Carol in an excited way pulled Candy aside and said, "Come on, we're going to the courthouse. This is historic and you need to see it."

So they ran past the pecan tree in the Chisholms' side yard, across the Hightowers' front yard that faced Summit Street, down the embankment behind the Community House and over to the Methodist Church, which was next door to the courthouse. On the south side of the church, they found an outdoor alcove with a perfect view of the courthouse steps where Dr. King was just stepping up to give a short speech. Carol and Candy were enthralled.

After his speech, Dr. King told the local Black people to line up and go inside to register to vote. Candy and Carol could see in their faces that they felt honored to be led in registering by the most famous Civil Rights leader in America.

Although there was not a Klan rally that day, two local Klansmen in full white robes and hoods stood across the street from the courthouse. Dr. Tom Dulin, superintendent of Winona Public Schools, remembers seeing them, but he said they took no action. "It was like they just wanted to get attention," Dulin said.

Carol Chisholm was an independent woman in many ways and she and Bob had a very equal marriage, at least by the standards of the time, but she let her husband take the lead in some ways and she never lied to him. So Candy wondered what would happen when her dad got home that night. He had been at the courthouse covering the event for his radio news, but Carol and Candy weren't sure if he had seen them there.

When Bob got home from work, Carol pulled her shoulders back and said, "Bob, I know you told us not to go to the courthouse today, but I felt Candy needed to see something so historic in our town."

Bob smiled affectionately and said, "Well, since there was no violence today, you made the right decision. I'm glad y'all came down to watch. It *was* a historic event, and Candy *did* need to see it."

FLASHBACK: CANDY JUSTICE

I had also been with my mother when I was 5 years old, and we found ourselves in the middle of a Ku Klux Klan daylight demonstration in Demopolis, Alabama, where my grandparents and aunt and uncle lived. My mother was in Rutledge's Drugstore drinking Cokes with her friends while I played with other children nearby in the park. Suddenly, lots of cars converged on the streets around the park and out of those cars jumped people in white robes with pointed hoods with eye and mouth holes cut out.

Despite my young age, I knew immediately it was something bad even though I had never heard of the Ku Klux Klan. But I was not afraid because they, of course, were not bothering the white children playing in the park. Instead, they were running up to Black people on the sidewalks, getting in their faces and screaming hateful things at them. I watched the Black people running for their lives, many of them crying out for mercy, and the men in white robes laughing and trying to frighten them more. Even as a 5-year-old, I knew that I was watching pure evil. As my mother came outside and

Martin Luther King in his coffin two years after the March Against Fear. Courtesy Special Collections, University of Memphis Library.

put her arm around me, we watched as the white robed men got back in their cars and drove away.

When I became an adult, I thanked my mom many times for letting me see that horrible Klan demonstration and for defying my dad to take me to hear Dr. King speak on the Winona courthouse steps. It was an education you can't get from a history book or a TV documentary. And as my mother liked to say about certain things, those experiences were good for my character.

A Friend to the Black Community

Bob and Carol would never have called themselves liberals, but that's what they were when it came to race relations and some other issues. They were Republicans in a time when the Democratic Party in Mississippi was dominated by staunch segregationists like

Senators John Stennis and Big Jim Eastland, and Jamie Whitten, who represented Mississippi in the U.S. House of Representatives for 53 years.

The Chisholms supported Rubel Phillips, a life-long Democrat, who ran unsuccessfully for governor of Mississippi twice as a Republican — in 1963 and 1967. He was only the third Republican since 1877 to run for governor in Mississippi. The Chisholm family was sitting in front of the TV on the night before the 1967 election when Phillips declared that Black people should have equal rights. Bob said, "That is going to lose Rubel a lot of white votes and probably lose him the election, but I'm proud of him for saying that publicly. He did the right thing." Carol agreed. Rubel Phillips lost that election to John Bell Williams, a conservative Democrat, who was a strong advocate for states' rights and racial segregation.

The Chisholms were politically active, but never demonstrated for civil rights by holding signs or leading voter registration drives. But many in the Black community in Winona said Bob did something better, something he was uniquely equipped to do, because of the widespread influence of his radio station.

Miss Millie Mae Moore, whom the Chisholms had known for many years, told Candy a few years ago without prompting, as she was driving Miss Moore to the funeral of Betty Townsend, "Your daddy stood up for us Black folks — he was always on our side," Miss Moore said, and it meant the world to Candy to hear her say that.

On another trip a few years later, Candy was in a Winona store, and two African American women in line with her at the check-out asked if she was visiting from out of town. Candy told them she was there for her class reunion and that she grew up in Winona. They asked who her parents were and when she told them, their faces lit up in smiles. One woman said, "The radio station man! I remember him — he did a lot of good things."

The Chisholm family definitely believed in helping people with their physical needs. When asked by street people for money in Memphis, Carol would often take them to a grocery store and buy them multiple bags of groceries of their own choosing and then drive them home. And it nearly killed Carol when Black people acted subservient to her or any white person.

That was a time when Black people felt they had to go to a white person's back door, but Carol insisted they use the front door. And back then, Black people, if they were being given a ride by a white person, would sit in the back seat. Carol asked them to sit on the front seat with her. Those were not earth-shattering actions, but it was Carol's small way of conveying that she believed in racial equality.

Meeting physical need is important, of course, but Bob and Carol also taught their daughter by example that sometimes the greatest gift you can give people is human dignity — helping them feel they matter, that they have something to contribute to society, something worth listening to. Like the homeless man who Candy encountered on a very cold day in Memphis. He said, "You don't have on gloves. Here take mine. I haven't even worn them yet — they gave them to me at the shelter."

At first Candy said, "Oh, no, I couldn't take your gloves when you need them on a cold day." But then she saw in his face that it was important to him for her to accept his gift. Candy took the gloves, put them on and thanked him profusely, and he smiled proudly and walked off. She still has those gloves, which incidentally were NFL brand gloves, and she wears them regularly in the winter, and thinks of that generous man.

Many would say the two greatest gifts Bob and Carol gave to the Black community in Winona were truthful courageous news reporting and the dignity they needed and deserved. One way Bob accomplished that was by starting an afternoon news and features show called The Negro Activity Calendar.

To our modern ears that name may *not* seem to bestow dignity and respect, but in the early and mid-1960s before the word "Black" was widely used, "Negro" was considered the most respectful word to use for a Black person. Not to be confused with a similar word that was and is very much a derogatory term. When Stokely Carmichael shouted the phrase "Black Power" for the first time during a rally in Greenwood, Mississippi, in 1966, it was part of the trend of "Black" becoming the dominant identifier by 1969.

The Negro Activity Calendar was greatly embraced by the Black community in Winona. It was produced entirely by a group of African Americans, mostly women, and aired live from the WONA studio in mid-afternoon. There were announcements about accomplishments, but mostly the program described meetings and social events of interest to the Black community. Candy still remembers the look of pride and importance on the faces of the Activity Calendar announcers at the times Candy happened to be in the control room looking through glass into the studio.

FLASHBACK: CANDY JUSTICE

Even if J.J. Knox students had to settle for leftover books and school equipment from Winona High School, there were other things that Knox excelled in far beyond Winona High School. They had a world-class choral music program led by Dr. Samuel J. Winbush, who served in many educational positions at Knox, including librarian, football and basketball coach, band director and choir director. The J.J. Knox Choir was a source of pride for the whole town, not just that school, and the choir was invited to perform far and wide.

My favorite example of how special the relationship was between my dad and the Winona Black community took place on a cold night just before Christmas when I was a teenager. My parents and I were talking at the dinner table when suddenly we went silent at the most beautiful sound we had ever heard. It sounded like a band of angels was singing Silent Night.

We jumped up and ran for the front porch and found the entire J.J. Knox Choir facing our house and singing in our front yard, just for us — mostly for my dad. Ours was the only house they were caroling to. When they segued to "Joy to the World," my parents and I all had tears in our eyes. Having a personal concert in our yard by the magnificent J.J. Knox Choir, directed by the incredible Dr. Samuel J. Winbush, was probably the most spectacular surprise of my life.

President Franklin D. Roosevelt visits Tupelo to celebrate the first TVA city and lays the groundwork for Winona to receive a community center. Photo courtesy Tennessee Valley Authority.

Chapter 8

Desegregation Comes To Winona Public Schools

Probably the biggest myth about the integration of public schools in Winona was that the Black community was clamoring for it to happen. Nothing could be further from the truth. There was much cooperation between leaders of the Black and white communities, but the African American parents were understandably concerned about their children's happiness and safety.

Winona public schools, like many other schools in Mississippi and elsewhere, were under federal court orders in the fall of 1967, requiring them to bring an end to racially separate public schools. The Winona School Board was made up of five white men with varying opinions on racial integration, but they agreed that carrying out the court order in the middle of the school year would be chaotic. Leaders like school Superintendent Dr. Tom Dulin felt it was important to desegregate thoughtfully and methodically for the sake of both Black and white students and the teachers.

Bill Liston, who was the city attorney and represented the school board, worked for hundreds of hours to prepare Winona's legal case and made numerous trips to the federal courthouse in Oxford, Mississippi, to file desegregation plans and other legal documents. Liston was one of the unheralded heroes of the effort to peacefully and successfully integrate Winona schools.

"Bill Liston never asked for a penny for all that work," according to Dulin, who said others who helped were the two newsmen in Winona — *Winona Times* Editor Hembree Brandon and WONA Manager Bob Chisholm.

But nobody put in as many hours on the effort as the unpaid Winona School Board — Chairman George Harris, Chut Billingsley, Jimmy Stringer, Tom Tardy and Billy Box.

"In one month, the school board and I met 28 times, and the earliest any meeting ended was 2 a.m.," Dulin recalled. "When it was all settled, I went to another town and rented a motel room and slept for three days, only waking up long enough for two meals."

The task before Dulin and the school board had been to come up with a workable plan that would be approved by the federal judge, who had made it clear that he would not give Winona schools a time extension unless there was an excellent detailed plan to start the desegregation process in 1967 before full integration of the two Winona schools was achieved in the 1969-70 school year.

The final plan involved first moving some white teachers to Knox school and having some Black students enrolled at the white school during the 1968-69 school year.

Henrese Roberts was the first Knox student to transfer to Winona High School. There were many details to be worked out, and Dulin said willingness by Black parents — the Tally Bibbs, Henry Roberts, Tommy Bibbs and Ora Clark families —was key and involved much discussion and their final agreement to enroll their children at the white school.

"The federal judge had given us until a certain date at midnight to get all the details worked out, "Dulin recalled, "but at 11:45 we still didn't have everybody's agreement, but then at five until 12, we were able to call the judge and get approval of our plan."

But approval was just the beginning — there were still so many details to work out, both practical (like how to help the first African American students learn their way around their new school) and rules based on principle (such as Dulin's insistence that no teachers would be allowed to continue teaching at the integrated public school if they moved their own children to the newly formed private school in Winona.)

And for the coming year, two more unexpected heroes emerged. Ole Miss Professor Roscoe Boyer and Delta State Professor Douglas McDonald made numerous trips to Winona to conduct free workshops with Dulin, teachers and parents to help them make the desegregation process fair and smooth.

In the end, Winona's smooth and peaceful desegregation of public schools would be heralded by many other school systems and educators as a model to follow. But the greatest heroes of this story are the Black parents and children who were courageous enough to begin the very important move toward school unity in Winona.

FLASHBACK: CANDY JUSTICE

When I saw one of those students, Shirley Bibbs Spivey, at our 50th class reunion, we spent long hours talking, laughing and reminiscing before and after official reunion activities, and I told her she was one of my heroes because she was brave enough to take a chance and be one of the first African Americans at Winona High School. In her typical charming and gracious way, Shirley refused to take any credit for courage.

Instead, she spoke of the good education she got at her new school, all the fun we had our senior year and she said she always felt welcomed and accepted at Winona High School. All of which left me loving her even more than before. What a lady! What a friend!

FDR's Community House Gift to Winona

Perhaps the most misunderstood quote of an American president was Franklin Roosevelt's "The only thing we have to fear is fear itself," which many people believe was spoken as encouragement to Americans during World II. However, FDR actually spoke those words during his *first* inaugural address in 1933, eight years before America entered the Second World War.

Certainly, there was great fear among Americans in 1933, but instead of fearing war and invasion, Americans feared hunger, homelessness and unemployment. In 1933 at the height of the Great Depression, more than 12.8 million Americans were unemployed. Some cities had as much as 90 percent unemployment.

And for Black Americans, it was even worse. The federal government had laws that enforced segregation, with the Federal Housing Administration (FHA) refusing to insure or give loans to Black families or to white families who lived too close to Black families.

When FDR's first attempts to turn around the worst economic disaster in American history failed, he and Harry Hopkins, FDR's closest advisor and later Secretary of Commerce, came up with a new group of government programs to try to decrease unemployment and improve towns and cities through construction projects. The Works Progress Administration (WPA) was the largest and best known of the programs, and it employed 8.5 million people at the height of the Depression. The WPA workers built bridges, public buildings, parks and airports, including New York's LaGuardia Airport.

In Mississippi, 17 community houses were constructed by WPA workers in the mid to late 1930s. The Winona Community House at 113 Sterling was one of them and was admitted to the National Register of Historic places in 2009 after being initially nominated by long-time Winona dance teacher, Susan Allen. The Winona Community House was praised by historians for its local rock façade and Tudor architecture.

Anyone who grew up in Winona or lived there for any amount of time would probably have attended parties, dances, class reunions and art exhibits at the Community House, and many have checked out books from the library in adjacent space on the north side of the Community House. Many WPA community houses were initially built as libraries. Winona's library moved from the Community House to a nearby free-standing library building in recent years.

Decorating for the Junior/Senior Banquet was a time-honored and fun tradition at the Winona Community House, but on April 4, 1968, a national tragedy brought student laughter to an abrupt halt. The juniors were working on the decorations at the Community House when a classmate came by to tell them the news — Dr. Martin Luther King had been assassinated while standing on the balcony outside his second-floor room at the Lorraine Motel in Memphis, Tennessee. Dr. King was shot by a lone gunman, who was later identified as James Earl Ray.

It seemed to many of the students like a nightmare that would never end. In less than five years, there had been so many assassinations and racial murders. Among them: President John F. Kennedy assassinated in Dallas; NAACP field secretary Medgar Evers gunned down in his own driveway in Jackson, Mississippi; four young African American girls murdered in a bombing of a Baptist Church in Birmingham; Young civil rights workers James

Chaney, Andrew Goodman and Michael Schwerner shot dead in Neshoba County, Mississippi, by the Ku Klux Klan; civil rights activist Malcolm X assassinated by a Muslim rival in Los Angeles; and James Meredith, who was shot but not killed during his March Against Fear in North Mississippi.

On April 4, 1968, at the Winona Community House, nobody could have known that in just two months, Bobby Kennedy would be shot to death in a Los Angeles hotel by a man who didn't like RFK's policy favoring Israel. Segregationist Alabama Governor George Wallace would follow a few years later during an assassination attempt that left him paralyzed the rest of his life. Of course, many other non-famous people had been hurt or killed because of the color of their skin or because of their beliefs, but it was leaders who some students were most thinking of that night.

Despite the shocking news about Dr. King, all of the students went back to decorating for the Junior-Senior Banquet — including their friend and classmate, Shirley Bibbs, who was the only African American in their junior class.

As they numbly continued with decorating, one student recalls thinking: "Is this what our country has come to? That when we don't agree with leaders, we just kill them?"

FLASHBACK: CANDY JUSTICE

Before any of us ever expected to hear about an assassination while we were decorating for a party, the Winona Community House had just been a place of carefree fun. It was tradition that the eighth graders had their first ever dance there just before Christmas. Everybody in the eighth grade was invited and most attended. We were told to dress up for the occasion, and some, including me, were encouraged (forced) by our mothers to take ballroom dancing

World vs. Bob Chisholm

lessons from Mrs. Susan Allen in her dance studio at her home on Fairground Street. The lessons were fun — Pete Childers and I were dance partners, and we won the cha cha contest.

But as the big dance, known officially as the Eighth Grade Party, approached, a different reality set in for me. My mother told me she was making me a green velvet jumper with a white organdy blouse, and it was indeed a beautiful outfit. She bought me new shoes and my first sheer stockings and told me I could wear a tiny bit of make-up.

I promptly told her that I would *not* be going to the dance. She promptly told me I certainly *was* going to the dance.

I told my mom I wasn't going because nobody would want to dance with me. My dad entered the argument by saying that *every* boy at the party would want to dance with me. I told him as respectfully as I could muster that he didn't know what he was talking about — I was too tall and gangly, not pretty and no boy in his right mind would ask me to dance.

My parents sweetly told me they were sorry I felt that way, but nonetheless, I was going to the dance in my green velvet dress. Case closed.

The most frightening part of this particular party was that Mrs. Allen and our parents insisted that we do it according to proper old-fashioned etiquette, where the girls would line up on one side of the Community House in firing squad style (my words not theirs), and the boys would line up on the other side of the room. The music would start and then the boys would walk toward us and ask somebody to dance. As the boys walked across that vast divide, I wanted to turn and run out the door, but my mother was a chaperone, and I knew she would stop me.

It was truly unbearable to watch those smiling boys head toward us. It seemed like slow motion to me. It is no exaggeration to say that I had never been as shocked in my life as I was when I was asked for that first dance by Jackie Austin, the most popular boy in our class. And I think every eighth-grade boy asked me to dance at some point that Cinderella evening. It was the most fun I had ever had in my short life, though it certainly did not permanently raise my low self-esteem. Even when I was a senior and was elected cheerleader, I assumed there had been a mistake in counting the ballots.

Twenty years later at a class reunion, I thanked Jackie for asking me to dance first on that socially terrifying night in eighth grade. He laughed and said he didn't remember asking me first, but suggested we mark the occasion by having a dance at the class reunion. And those two dances, 20 years apart, were, to my recollection, the only two times Jackie and I ever danced together. But to this day, I still think of Jackie Austin as one of the heroes in my life.

The Mule Train Comes to Winona

Four days before he was assassinated, Dr. Martin Luther King announced at the National Cathedral in Washington, D.C., that he would be bringing a poor people's campaign to the U.S. capitol. He told the crowd that he had recently been to Marks, Mississippi, which is in Quitman County, then the poorest county in the United States, and that he had seen hundreds of Black children walking the streets with no shoes to wear and with stomachs distended from lack of proper nutrition. [Editor's note: Marks is also the birthplace of Fred W. Smith the future founder of FedEx].

Courtesy Special Collections, University of Memphis Libraries.
Martin Luther King

That's why he planned to begin the Poor People's Campaign in Marks. The idea was to bring thousands of people from all over the nation to D.C., but the emphasis would not be on just the problems of poor Black people. Rather Dr. King and his Southern Christian Leadership Conference wanted a multi-racial coalition of poor people — the goal was to unite all ethnicities, including poor Hispanic, Native American, Asian, African American and white people. He wanted a movement that sought economic justice through nonviolent methods.

Supporters of the campaign came to D.C. from many locations throughout the U.S., most of them traveling by car or busloads. However, one campaign route from Marks to Washington stood out from the rest because the people traveled in covered wagons pulled by mules, as a symbol of poor sharecroppers. Hand-written slogans on the cloth coverings of the 15 wagons included "Jesus was a Poor Man," "I Have Seen the Promise Land" and "Feed the Poor."

Many young people were among the travelers, but the parents of some others would not allow them to go because they feared that if Dr. King could be killed, their children might also be killed.

When the Mule Train left Marks on May 13, 1968, the passengers ranged in age from 8 months to 70 years old. Wagon train stops in Mississippi included Eupora, Grenada, Duck Hill and Winona. In some towns, the mule train was met with curiosity, not violence. In others, armed police or sheriff's deputies stopped the wagon train from entering the towns. In the worst-case scenarios, the travelers were beat with the butts of rifles, some of their faces permanently disfigured.

In Winona, the mule train passengers were met with a much-needed dose of kindness and compassion. Dr. Tom Dulin, the superintendent of Winona Public Schools, remembers well when the wagon train reached Winona. He talked with leaders in the Black community, including Arthur Norwood, Tally Bibbs, Tommy Bibbs and Ora Clark, and they came up with a plan.

"They had gotten beat up in Grenada, and they were hurt and tired," Dulin recalled. "They just needed a few days to recover. We talked them into parking the wagons and mules on the football field at Knox School (then the Black school in Winona), and we fed them in the school cafeteria from Friday until Monday."

For the safety of the travelers, Dulin and other Winona community leaders thought it was best to keep the protesters' whereabouts secret.

"I didn't tell anyone they were staying in Winona," Dulin said, "not even the police."

From Mississippi, the mule train went through Alabama and on to Atlanta, where the entire mule train and riders boarded a train bound for Alexandria, Virginia. On June 19, 1968, the mule train crossed the Potomac River and rolled into D.C., joining thousands of others from around the country, who lived for six weeks in an encampment called Resurrection City on the National Mall. Their Poor People's Campaign has been credited with helping to bring about Congressional action to create nutrition and housing programs for the poor.

Candy Chisholm Justice, age 20. Photo courtesy Candy Chisholm Justice

Chapter 9

Candy's Life of Crime

Anyone searching for optimism, happiness, exhilaration and glee between 1968 and 2000, might have found what they were looking for — at least temporarily — at concerts and half-time shows at which a group of young adults calling themselves Up With People offered singing, dancing, hope, and joy. They branded themselves as specializing in positivity and multiculturalism expressed through music at venues ranging from an inauguration of a U.S. President to a celebration of the fall of the Berlin Wall.

Candy saw them perform at Fulton Chapel at Ole Miss when she was a freshman during the 1969-70 school year. That was before they ever dreamed they would end up doing five half-time shows during Super Bowls between 1976 and 1986. And before *The Simpsons* writers created a group named "Hooray for Everything," which parodied Up With People.

Not everyone found the performance group uplifting. The *City-County Observer* in Evansville Indiana, once described the group as a "cultish utopian ideology" that was funded by corporate America as part of a propaganda effort to "discredit liberal counterculture."

The performance at Ole Miss that Candy attended was entertaining in an overly perky sort of way, but during the grand finale, something unexpected happened — a small group of African American Ole Miss students calmly but seriously walked onto the stage and the music ended abruptly. The protesters didn't shout or do anything aggressive or violent, but they were clearly trying to make a point about racial inequality. The audience just sat there.

Then Campus Security officers rushed in and tried to arrest the protestors, most of whom ran off stage and out of the building. Candy went back to her dormitory room, having no idea that within a few hours she would be committing a felony.

Early the next morning, her dorm phone rang, and a male voice addressed her by name, saying he was with the FBI, and they needed to talk to her at the Alumni House on campus right away. Candy wasn't frightened, but wondered what this summons was all about.

When she got there, two FBI agents sat her down at a table where several 8 x 10 photos were spread out before her. Nobody asked her if she had been at the Up with People show the night before. They didn't tell her how they knew she was there. Candy thought that was odd since the show was free and there was no sign-in involved.

Candy remembered the students in the photos as being among the protestors on stage the night before but said nothing. The FBI agent asked if she recognized anyone among them. She had only a few seconds to decide if she would lie or tell the truth. Lying won. She said no, she didn't recognize any of them.

But, of course, she had immediately recognized one of the students in the photos, just as she had recognized her when she walked on the stage during the protest. It was Henrese Roberts. Candy and Henrese were both from Winona, and they both went to Winona High School the year before the school was fully desegregated. Candy also knew her from Ole Miss, where the two coeds always said hi when they saw each other on campus.

But Candy was not about to tell the FBI agents any of that. They were clearly trying to get her to identify Henrese so she could be arrested or punished in some other way. But as far as Candy was concerned, Henrese and the other African American students were just exercising their First Amendment rights to peacefully assemble and protest. But the FBI wasn't buying what Candy was selling.

One of the agents picked up Henrese's photo and said, "Do you recognize this person?" Candy said, "No." He held the picture closer to Candy's face and said, "Are you sure you don't recognize her?" Candy's answer was, "No, I've never seen her before."

It wasn't until about five years ago that Candy learned that lying to the FBI is a felony, but if she had known that back then, she still would have lied.

Candy says she has respect for the FBI of today, imperfect though it may be sometimes, like any group of human beings. But in 1969, the FBI was still under the iron fist of J. Edgar Hoover, who had been FBI director for 37 years and had abused that power for all kinds of malign purposes, including helping Richard Nixon establish his "enemies list." Hoover also used his power to intimidate and harass political dissenters and activists. Back then, lying to J. Edgar Hoover's boys when they were trying to trample on a student's First Amendment rights was a no brainer to a journalism major like Candy.

FLASHBACK: CANDY JUSTICE

It was many years later before I found out what happened to Henrese and the other students who protested that night in Fulton Chapel. I had naively assumed nothing had happened to her since I had *not* identified her to the FBI. But apparently somebody did. Twenty or more years later I saw an article in a Memphis newspaper about a man who had been one of those protestors. He and all the other student protesters had been expelled, but he had gone to another university and gotten a doctorate and was then working as a high administrator at Ole Miss.

I contacted him and told him my story. My family had moved to Memphis a few months after the protest, so I had not run into Henrese in our hometown in the intervening years. I asked the Ole Miss administrator about her, and he said the unfairness of the expulsion had had a big impact on Henrese's life. I asked if he could tell me how to contact her, but either he forgot to send me her address or didn't want to violate her privacy. Or maybe he didn't believe me. Who could blame him if he found my story far-fetched, that a white Ole Miss girl lied to the FBI to protect a Black student. I will always hope that Henrese didn't think I was the one who ratted her out to the FBI.

Arthur and Bob

In small Southern towns during the 1960s, close personal friendships between a Black man and a white man existed but were not common, though Ellis Hart and Giles Edwards in Winona immediately come to mind.

Bob Chisholm and Arthur Norwood got to know each other through their mutual desire to see Winona schools peacefully integrated. But that relationship, based on a common goal, grew into a truly personal friendship where the two men enjoyed each other's company immensely, laughing and talking about all kinds of things.

Arthur was a graduate of Rust College, earned a Master's Degree in administration from NYU and did post graduate work at Princeton, Columbia University and Mississippi State University. Despite being highly educated and having a prestigious career in education and administration, Arthur chose to come back to his hometown to help make it a better place for both Black and white citizens.

Bob, on the other hand, was a dropout after one year at a small, not-at-all prestigious college in Kentucky. He then went to radio school in Minneapolis, paying his bills by waiting tables in a restaurant owned and frequented by mobsters, who avoided sitting with their backs to the door, so they could shoot back if a rival gangster came in. Bob didn't admire the mobsters in most ways, but as a young, struggling waiter, he appreciated their generous tips. Which is why Bob for the rest of his life was always a big tipper, a habit he passed on to his daughter. It rubbed off on his wife, too. Carol was appalled when she was eating lunch at the City Café in Winona, and overheard at the next table, a diner saying to her friend, "You don't have to tip. I already left a dime for the girl."

• • • • • • • • • •

Arthur and Bob's friendship came to an abrupt heart-breaking end in March of 1970. Carol and Candy were both at home when Bob walked through the door with tears rolling down his cheeks.

"Arthur is dead," he said, choking on his tears. "They killed him."

"Who killed him?" my mom demanded angrily.

"All of the people who hated him and didn't want him helping Black people or changing things around here for the better. Arthur had a massive heart attack and died. He was only 44 years old."

"So nobody shot him or anything like that?" Carol clarified.

"No, but they might as well have. They fought him about everything good he accomplished and wanted to do. And his heart just couldn't take all the hate. He was a good man — he didn't deserve what they did to him."

Bob grieved long and hard for his friend, Arthur Norwood, and missed Arthur for the rest of his life.

• • • • • • • • • •

Recently, Candy came upon some of Bob's papers and among them was a eulogy for Mr. Norwood from his funeral on April 1, 1970.

Arthur M. Norwood — In Memoriam

It is not given to any of us to comprehend the full extent of our Creator's will in this life: why one man's feet should be set on a certain path, those of his brother on yet another.

Our friend is gone from among us, and our hearts are sad. It is difficult to understand why the path that was his to walk should have so soon come to an end. But those of us who knew him can reflect that many men have lived longer, journeyed farther, had more opportunities for service, yet never managed to accomplish a hundredth as much as he did.

He had that rare ability to find friends in every stratum of our society, from the poorest to the leaders in education, religion, government and business. And he had that even rarer ability to persuade them to help in whatever worthwhile endeavor he was interested in — and they were many.

Because he himself had known firsthand many of life's hardships, he had an insight, an understanding, a sympathy for human needs that few men ever achieve.

He never wasted time bemoaning the fact that he wasn't born rich. Many is the time he acknowledged with pride and love his gratitude to his father and mother for what they meant to his life, for instilling in him a love for his fellow man.

He never doubted those precepts that served him so well; that there is no indignity in honest work; that there is no shame in seeking help from friends; that one's principles are never compromised by sacrificing an immediate result to win a greater victory that lies yet ahead.

He had, in his day, known indignity and injustice — but he refused to belittle himself by hating those few who could not accept his friendship because his skin was a different color.

Even in those times when he knew frustration and disappointment, I never knew him to harbor bitterness and resentment. He simply accepted the situations and began looking for another way to get done what needed to be done. He didn't always find that way, but he tried — and he kept on trying.

He could have easily turned his back and gone elsewhere, for more money and fewer problems. But he chose to stay here at home with people he knew and loved, where he felt the opportunities for service were greatest.

There are many of you who know far more fully than I the scope of the good he did: those little acts of everyday kindness; the generosity he showed to everyone; his ability to be there when he was needed; his willingness to tackle any worthwhile task without making excuses.

All these came from the heart, and they will be remembered equally as long as the larger deeds: his helping needy students to go to school; getting medicine or food or clothing for someone who couldn't buy them; finding jobs for those who needed them; working to improve community relations and promoting better understanding; and the many other areas in which he felt it was his duty and obligation to help however he could. He seldom waited until he was asked, but went ahead and did what he could.

The schools to which he devoted 20 years of his life, were his first love…and the contributions he made there will go on and on. But I think perhaps the lessons he best will be remembered for were not taught in the schools, but in the everyday walks of life as he gave so open-heartedly of himself.

Even though time was not allotted to him to accomplish all he would have wished, the many things he did accomplish set him a notch above those who settled for a less-demanding route.

The lives he affected, the futures he changed, the friends he made: these are a reward, a tribute, a memorial he would have prized above all others.

Because he was concerned, because he cared, perhaps many paths will be less arduous as a result of his having traveled this way. Who knows how many yet to come will face fewer obstacles because he chose not to content himself with being mediocre or taking the easy way.

We, his friends, will miss him. All our lives have been altered because, for these moments in time, our worlds came in contact with his. When a friend dies, a part of us dies with him. Yet as long as there is memory, a part of our friend will live in us.

Mad at Bob? Get in Line and Take a Number!

Everybody in Winona seemed to either like and admire Bob Chisholm … or hate him with a passion.

One Winona businessman made it known around town that he was willing to pay as much as $25,000 to anyone who would "run Bob Chisholm out of town." When Bob got wind of this, he phoned the businessman and told him, "Hell, for $10,000, I'll pack up and leave!" He wouldn't have left, of course, for any amount of money. Bob had too much integrity and determination to run away. But it gave Bob a chuckle to ruffle the man's feathers. It was typical of Bob to face detractors head on but do it in a disarmingly funny way.

It infuriated his enemies far more effectively than a shouting match would have.

Chief Engineer and Announcer Maurice Gooch remembers a time during the Morning Edition of the News broadcast when a local man walked into the radio station and asked where he could find Bob Chisholm. As Gooch was explaining that Bob was on the air in the adjacent studio, Maurice noticed the man had a gun stuck in his belt. Warily, he asked the visitor why he needed to see Bob.

"I don't like some of the things he's been saying on the news," the man said. "So, I aim to kill him."

For the next 10 minutes, the shaken announcer asked the man to take a seat and Maurice quietly tried to dissuade him from doing anything rash. "I finally figured out," Gooch said later, "that he was unhappy but not really angry. While the man was distracted, though, I got a two by four piece of wood as a precaution."

When Bob came into the control room after the news, Gooch introduced him to the man and explained he was upset and had said he wanted to kill Bob, who remained calm and invited the man to go with him to City Café, where he bought the man a cup of coffee.

When Bob returned to the station an hour or so later, he told his relieved engineer that the man just wanted someone to listen to him. The man never came to the radio station again. Bob Chisholm was good at judging who really meant harm and who just needed to be heard. He never over-reacted.

A courageous reporter makes a lot of enemies but also accumulates many admirers. Bob and Carol Chisholm could barely pay their bills during their 12 years at WONA, but they were paid generously in the respect and admiration they got from most of the people of Winona. A price can't be attached to that.

Some people might have said Bob Chisholm didn't always play well with others. He didn't. He had little tolerance for closed-minded people, unethical people, racists or for those who tried to cheat others or to hide things. Actually, that's not right. He had <u>no</u> tolerance for those kinds of people.

But, then again, not everyone played well with Bob. People who tried to hide things didn't like Bob. He was a pragmatic idealist. He wanted to see people and events in their best light, but he also understood there were wrongs in the world that needed to be exposed and righted, as well as people and ideals that deserved to be protected. He was never a muckraker.

He didn't go after people to hurt them or to make them look foolish. He did, however, pursue public officials or citizens who did things in secret that might be, at the least, self-serving, and at the worst, harmful to the city or to other people. Bob had no tolerance for injustice. He only tolerated the truth.

Sometimes Bob discovered truth in unexpected places. Bryan's younger brother, Joe Cottingham, was a young entrepreneur. When he was 10 years old, Joe operated a "sno-cone stand" in downtown Winona. A local businessman provided the financing, and Joe ran the operation, setting up in strategic locations and making and selling the sno-cones.

He was always on the lookout for a good location that had high walking traffic but did not block the streets. There was a small, dead-end alley between the radio station building and a local women's clothing store. Joe decided this was a perfect location. He went to the store owner and asked if he could set up his stand in the alley next to the store.

The owner, who happened to be on the Board of Aldermen, told Joe the alley was owned by the city. Appreciating Joe's enthusiasm and wanting to encourage his resourcefulness, the store owner told him he should go before the Board and ask permission to set up his business. "In fact," he told Joe, "The Board is having a special meeting tonight. Why don't you come and make your case?" Bryan was at the station at the time, so Joe went up to tell him about the invitation. Bob overheard Joe's news but was perplexed by one small detail. As far as he, or anyone else in Winona knew, the Board did not have a public meeting scheduled for that night.

Bob immediately called Hembree Brandon, editor of the *Winona Times,* to see if he knew anything about the meeting. He didn't. The two newsmen decided the secret meeting probably had an equally secret agenda the public should know about. Promptly at seven o'clock, just as the meeting was called to order, Bob and Hembree walked in and took their seats, notebooks and pens poised to take down the pertinent details.

Contrary to their original plan for an agenda-packed secret meeting, the only matter the visibly uncomfortable aldermen considered was the request by a young man to locate a sno-cone machine in a public alley.

After a short discussion, the members congratulated Joe on being a go-getter and approved his request with a collective smile. A motion to adjourn was immediately offered and approved as the aldermen hastily gathered their undisclosed notes and departed without answering any questions from the two inquisitive journalists who had turned the aldermen's private gathering into a public meeting. Whatever was on the original agenda was never revealed, and apparently was not taken up again.

Public scrutiny has a way of dissuading secrecy. The Board was not happy to see Bob and Hembree and never discovered how they found out about the meeting. Sixty years later, the source is now revealed for the first time — 10-year-old Joe Cottingham.

That was not the only time the Winona Board of Mayor and Aldermen tried to pull some shenanigans. The Board of Supervisors and Board of Aldermen met on a schedule, and Bob and Hembree attended every meeting.

But the two boards came up with an idea they thought would thwart the two newsmen — the two boards normally met on different nights but they decided to start meeting on the same night so Bob and Hembree could only cover one meeting. Apparently, the boards didn't realize that Bob and Hembree were close friends and didn't see each other as competitors but as fellow journalists.

So when the two boards began meeting the same night, Hembree went to one and Bob went to the other, and after the meetings they got together and shared notes. So it was the Board members who were thwarted, not the two newsmen. Full coverage of the meetings was made public by Hembree's newspaper and Bob's radio station.

The vast majority of Chisholm haters were elected officials who were determined to keep some of their actions secret, especially illegal and unethical actions. They used intimidation and other threats to try to keep their secrets secret. Mostly they were bluffing — that's why Bob and his family didn't live in constant fear and usually took death threats with a grain of salt. At an early age, Bob's daughter Candy figured out that people who were really going to kill you probably wouldn't call and announce their intentions in advance.

However, sometimes the hate directed at Bob became very frightening. A man called Bob and told him while hunting he had overheard two men complaining about Bob. It wasn't the usual bravado and big talk. This time the men were seriously discussing the idea that Bob should be "taken care of…for good."

The caller did not know who the two conspirators were, but the overheard conversation scared him enough to cause him to call Bob and warn him that his life might be in danger. Nobody could figure out who the potential murderers were, but Bob was certainly on guard for a while.

••••••••••

The County Board of Supervisors in many Mississippi counties were rife with corruption. Supervisors were elected officials whose job was to direct the building of roads and other physical needs outside the city limits. The problem was that they sometimes used public funds to do something in their personal interest, such as build improved roads that only led to their own houses.

Kickbacks were also common crimes among elected supervisors, who sometimes made illegal deals with businesses selling building materials and equipment. There was a case where a supervisor allegedly used public funds to buy a large number of concrete culverts that were supposed to be used to build small bridges over creeks and gullies. The supervisor allegedly took a kickback from the culvert manufacturer and left all the culverts in a field with weeds growing over them.

As far back as anyone could remember, corruption among county supervisors was just accepted, not because most people who lived in the county approved of it, but because there was no recourse. There was nobody to complain to who would actually take action against corrupt supervisors.

When Bob Chisholm came along and started reporting on the corruption, the criminal activity didn't entirely go away, but people found out what was going on, which did at least make crooked supervisors slow down a bit for fear of not getting re-elected. When

Bob and Hembree started covering the misdeeds of the supervisors, anonymous death threats on the phone to Brandon and Chisholm took an upturn.

The Winona Board of Aldermen, the city's governing board, had a big share of Chisholm and Brandon haters, too. They were less likely to engage in the high level of corruption common among the Board of Supervisors, but they had plenty of actions they preferred for the public not to know about, too. For example, giving raises to themselves or other city employees who the public might think didn't deserve more money.

And the thing about news coverage of small-town government is that you don't just have citizens reading about controversial decisions in the newspaper like you would in a big city and then cussing about them to friends. No, there is a lot more grassroots accountability in a small town.

If a small-town elected official does something the public doesn't like and it is reported in the local media, those elected officials have to face their angry constituents as they pass them on the street or see them at church. Or they get angry phone calls from people who are on a first-name basis with the politicians. And those angry citizens usually don't make anonymous threats — they actually show up on election day and make their opinions known with their votes.

Friends and Spies

Those were the days before Mississippi had open meetings and open records laws, which require that all government meetings and public records, except those specifically exempt, have to be open to the public, including members of the press. Those state laws are collectively called "Sunshine Laws."

Mississippi's 1975 open meetings law was extremely weak, however, and was not strengthened until 1981. But even without Sunshine Laws, the Winona Board of Aldermen and Board of Supervisors didn't dare openly declare their meetings off limits to the press and the public, not that members of the public often attended. But people knew that Bob and Hembree would be there on the public's behalf and would report the news in the newspaper and on the radio.

A few years later, Bob's accountant and close friend, Billy Flowers, was elected to the Winona Board of Aldermen. Billy was a fine man, who would never do anything illegal or unethical, but that didn't mean he didn't privately from time to time feed Bob and Hembree information that some of the other aldermen didn't want the press or the public to know about. One of Billy's twin sons, Jerry Flowers, grew up to be elected and re-elected mayor of Winona.

FLASHBACK: CANDY JUSTICE

One of the members of the Board of Aldermen was also a civics teacher at Winona Junior High School. He really hated my dad for something WONA had reported on the Morning Edition of the News. When this teacher couldn't figure out a way to get back at my father directly, he took the cowardly approach of taking it out on me, a seventh grader at the time.

Numerous times, the teacher would do things in class to berate or embarrass me. Finally, I had had enough and went home at the end of the day and told my parents what the alderman/teacher had done to me in class. I have always looked back with affection and admiration at my dad's response to my complaint. My parents listened sympathetically. Then Daddy said, "Baby, that was unfair of him to treat you like that because he was mad at me, but there is nothing we can do about it. You'll just have to live with it."

I didn't argue. I knew my dad was right.

The Chisholm Family Singers

There are musical families and then there were the Chisholms. In fairness, one of the Chisholms did have a nice singing voice, but it wasn't Bob or Candy. Carol liked to reminisce about the fun of singing alto in the All-Girl Choir at the Methodist Church in her hometown of Demopolis, Alabama.

Bob never sang in the shower or hummed while he worked, though he loved listening to music and playing it on his radio station WONA. But he sang loud and boisterously in one place and one place only — the car when the family went on a road trip to visit grandparents or on one of the few times they went to the beach for a vacation.

Candy taught Bob to sing the Mickey Mouse Club song, which every kid and most adults knew the words to. But the songs Bob taught Candy, she had never heard anywhere else. Songs like: "Alice Where are You Going?" A popular camp song that dates back to pre-television years. It is about a girl named Alice, who has "legs like toothpicks" and a neck "like a giraffe" who goes upstairs to take a bath amid fears she might slip down the drain. The song is an obvious reference to Lewis Carroll's popular children's book, *Alice in Wonderland*.

After nearly a lifetime of thinking her dad's sing-along was made up of *his* songs, that were his alone, a quick computer search recently educated Candy on those songs. Turns out most of them are country/western songs that Candy never came across because she generally doesn't like country/western music. But she loved them when sung by her dad and herself. Candy's favorite of her Dad's songs was *Ragtime Cowboy Joe:*

> *He always sings,*
> *Raggedy music to his cattle as he swings,*
> *Back and forward on a horse — a pretty good horse —*
> *that was syncopated gated and was such a funny meter to the roar of his repeater,*
> *How they run, when the fellow waves his gun,*
> *Because the Western folks all know:*
> *He's a high fallutin', root 'n tootin' son of a gun from Arizona,*
> *Ragtime cowboy — talk about your cowboy — Ragtime Cowboy Joe!*

The version of *Cowboy Joe* that Candy found online was too twangy for her taste, but she really liked a lively George Jones/Jerry Reed version of *Ragged But Right,* another of Bob's and Candy's car songs. There was even a Jerry Garcia version on YouTube. Candy is not a Grateful Dead fan, but she discovered that she absolutely loved the Jerry Garcia Acoustic Band.

It is funny and ironic that the Jones/Reed version of *Ragged But Right* would have been G rated, but the one Candy sang in the car with her dad when she was 6 or 7 was the PG version, maybe even PG-13, with talk of gambling, being a thief and getting high. The George Jones version and Jerry Garcia version mention a "little baby girl playing around at my feet" while in Bob's version, it was just "a pretty girl."

Candy was an adult before she realized that one of the songs her dad had taught her was a risqué drinking song:

Ragged But Right
I just called up to tell you that I'm ragged, but right,
A thief, a gambler, high every night,
I eat a porterhouse steak three times a day for my board,
More than any ordinary guy can afford,
I've got a big electric fan to keep me cool while I sleep,
A pretty girl to play around with my feet.
I'm a rambler, a gambler, high every night,
I just called up to tell you that I'm ragged but right.

•••••••••

Though Carol only joined in when Bob and Candy sang the Mickey Mouse Club theme song, she and Candy had their own family singers thing going on. They loved the movie musicals of the 1950s and 60s, like *The Music Man, Singing in the Rain, Oklahoma* and *South* Pacific, and there was a running joke between them when they were sitting in a restaurant, library or other stayed location that it would be a good time to jump up on a table and break into song, as they do improbably in movie musicals.

FLASHBACK: CANDY JUSTICE

In the car sometimes, my mom and I sang, with her nice voice taking the alto and me singing poorly on the melody part. Our very favorite was the counterpoint duet in *The Music Man* — which was sung in the movie by the Buffalo Bills and Shirley Jones. I always sang *Lida Rose* with my mom singing *Will I Ever Tell You?*

We sang that counterpoint duet in private for 45 years, the last time being just a few hours before Mama died peacefully in her sleep on January 16, 2013, when she was 85. I had a feeling it might be our last night together, so I turned on the *Music Man* CD with our duet. *Lida Rose* starts first, so I sang that part and when *Will I Tell You* was supposed to come in, I pointed to my mom like "your turn."

Mama was too weak at that point to sing out loud, but I knew she was singing in her mind, and she smiled a weak version of her beautiful smile. I slept with her in her bed at her home that last night. What I wouldn't give to sing *Lida Rose/Will I Tell You* with my mama one more time!

The Brandon–Chisholm Coalition

In the 1960s, there was a secret path that led from the backdoor of a house on Jones Street to the back door of 108 Webster Street. The secret path may still be there, for all we know. Candy never knew anybody to use it except Jean, Hembree and Steve Brandon when they needed a shortcut to the home of Carol, Bob and Candy Chisholm. Steve Brandon, a Jackson, Mississippi, attorney now, but a little boy then, remembers those rendezvous well:

"I remember playing on the floor of your house on Friday nights and reading books on the couch, while your parents and my parents ate dinner, played Scrabble and laughed and laughed and laughed. The TV in your house was towards the back of your den, close to the kitchen door.

While our parents entertained themselves, I watched The Brady Bunch, The Partridge Family, Room 222 and The Odd Couple. After Love American Style, we walked back to our house by taking a shortcut through your backyard. Bob and Carol had the best senses of humor! Such wonderful and special people!"

A lot of that laughter between the Brandons and the Chisholms came from the inside jokes among them. Bob nearly always called Hembree "H.B. Henry." Bob and Hembree had private nicknames for many of the local leaders who opposed the strong reporting both men did. One prominent man in Winona, who considered himself a pillar of the community and the Baptist church, actually was quite a hypocrite, so Bob and Hembree always referred to him in private as "The Right Reverend (his first name)."

Carol and Candy privately called Bob's stingy boss "Ebenezer," and they called their landlord behind his back "Biggy Rat," because he was always chomping on a cigar like the cartoon character by that name.

Hembree, as editor of the *Winona Times*, and Bob, manager and newsman at radio station WONA, should by all rights have been competitors at best and enemies at worse, but instead were absolute kindred spirits and partners in truth telling, and were close friends. Jean was Candy's beloved English teacher in 8th grade and the director of the senior play, along with their beloved senior English teacher, Brenda Taylor.

The senior play was Agatha Christie's *The Mousetrap*, in which Candy played the nasty Mrs. Boyle, who was murdered by Rick Read at the end of the second act.

Even though Candy was much, much older than Steve and Lisa Brandon, she loved them and enjoyed entertaining them when their families were together, and Candy happened to be home. Steve bestowed on Candy a high honor in recent years by telling her he had an older-girl crush on Phyllis Townsend, Diane Dotson and Candy — putting her in lofty company!

The World's Best Workaholic Dad

It's just not fair to compare a father of the 1950s and 1960's with a father of today. Fathers of that earlier time didn't love their children less than fathers of today, but compared to the best fathers of today, they definitely spent little or no one-on-one time with their children (with a few notable exceptions perhaps).

Few dads back then came home from work at exactly five o'clock, changing into casual clothes and then going out in the yard to play with their kids. If they had, the kids would have wondered, "Why is *he* out here? Dads don't play Kick the Can and Red Rover." And when the kids were playing their favorite game, "Pretend," what part would your father play? The pretend father of the pretend family?"

In the 50s and 60s, dads came home from work, sat down in a comfortable chair and read the newspaper or watched TV. Or took a nap while their wives cooked dinner. Of course, they did — fathers had worked all day and were tired and just wanted a little peace and quiet. Is that too much to ask?

Of course, mothers had worked all day, too — either at their own jobs or at home with very few modern conveniences like microwave ovens and dishwashers, many without washing machines and dryers and in the Chisholm house without air conditioning.

Carol had a washing machine, but if it was rainy or too cold to hang the laundry on the outside clothesline, she would have to drive the wet clothes to the town's only laundromat and sit there while the clothes dried. No late afternoon nap, newspaper reading or TV watching for her.

Moms were tired at the end of the day, but it never occurred to them not to cook dinner and maybe run a load of laundry while they cooked and took care of the kids. It's what mothers did, and still do in many families. And if you lived in a small town like Winona, a mother would *not* say, "I'm tired, let's go out for supper" or "Let's pick up some fast food."

They didn't say it, mostly because there were no restaurants open at night unless you count The Mug and Cone or Satellite Drive In. And what self-respecting mother of the 50s and 60s would go to a teen hang-out and order hamburgers and French fries to take home for her family's supper? That would just be weird, right? Mothers were supposed to make a meat and vegetables dinner or at the very least, make homemade hamburgers and French fries for the family.

Bob always came home for supper, and there was lively conversation around the dinner table. After supper, he did one of two things: he went out again to cover the Board of Alderman meeting or other newsworthy events, or he read the two or three newspapers they took at home, watched a little television and went to bed about 8, sometimes earlier.

Saturdays and Sundays weren't much different, except that Bob did have a little more free time that he could have spent with Candy doing whatever some dads did with their kids. But Candy was too busy playing with the neighborhood kids to notice that he didn't do anything with her. The other kids' dads didn't either.

Carol, for the most part, accepted that her husband was not going to take part in family outings. Bob didn't even go to church with them, which Carol mildly complained about by saying to Candy, "I'm just the Widow Chisholm taking her little girl to church."

It was a running joke, but she did yearn for them to go to church as a family, not that they were the only family in town where the father refused to go to church with his wife and children. Bob said he couldn't go to the Methodist Church with his family because he had to be at First Baptist Church, operating the remote equipment that broadcast the Baptist service on WONA in real time every

Sunday morning. Carol contended that he could have made somebody else on the station staff do it but to no avail.

On rare occasions, Carol would succeed in "guilting" Bob into doing something family-like. She talked him into going on a picnic one time, and he wore his ubiquitous dark suit, white dress shirt and dark tie and looked like he couldn't wait to get away and go back to work.

Another time, Candy was in her bedroom and could hear her parents arguing in the next room. Her mom was telling Bob he only had one child — so the least he could do was spend some time alone with her every once in a while. The term "quality time" had not been invented yet.

Bob went into Candy's room, of course wearing a suit and tie, and told her he was going to read her a story. They both felt very awkward while he read the book, but she knew he was trying to please her mother, so she played along. Candy would have much preferred for them to talk about politics and world events as they often did in their family.

There was only one other time during Candy's childhood that she remembers her dad initiating a one-on-one outing with her, and that time it seemed to be his idea (no argument with her mom preceded it).

On a Sunday afternoon, he asked Candy if she would like to take a walk with him. She thought that would be fun, so gladly said yes. This time it was *not* awkward, and they walked a long time, oddly including walking down the railroad tracks, which Bob said he and his brothers did when they were kids.

It was a beautiful day, and they talked easily about all kinds of things, though nothing heavy. It became a very happy memory for

Candy, although it needs to be said that she didn't expect that to ever happen again, and it didn't.

And by the way, he wore a dark suit and tie with a white dress shirt on their walk. Candy never saw him wear anything else until they moved to Memphis when she was a freshman at Ole Miss, at which time he suddenly discovered he liked wearing shorts on his days off, and more often on weekends, wearing baggy fatigue pants with multiple pockets that he bought at the Army Surplus Store.

So, Bob never played a board game with his daughter, only read a picture book to her once, didn't teach her to ride a bicycle or drive a car, never helped her build a science project or snowman and never wrote her a letter when she was away at college. So, you are feeling pretty sorry for Candy about now, right?

But the truth is Candy had a fantastic, fun, exciting childhood and all her parents' lives, she had an extremely close relationship with both of them. She was always fully aware that she was the luckiest kid in the world, even if she might sometimes have wished for store-bought clothes instead of clothes sewed by her mother. But how many kids are told they can drop in any time at their dad's workplace, especially when it is a radio station, and hang out as long as she wished. And how many only children have numerous cool "big brothers."

And though money was always very tight in the Chisholm family, Candy never left her dad's presence that he didn't say, "Baby, do you need some money?" and then he would slip her a quarter, and when she was older, it was a dollar. Even though her dad never went to church with his family, he never forgot to give Candy a quarter for the collection plate.

••••••••••

Because her mom was a talented amateur seamstress, probably no one thought she sewed for her daughter and herself out of necessity. In fact, a lot of people in Winona thought Bob owned the radio station and therefore was financially well off.

The truth was that Bob was the station manager, and thanks to him, WONA brought in a lot of advertising revenue, but he got a very small salary from the owner, who lived in another town. Bob and Carol sometimes could barely pay their bills.

When Candy was a senior in high school, some of her classmates came up with the idea that they would each pitch in $25 to have a big senior dance with a band, and all their classmates could attend. They proposed it to Candy, thinking her parents could easily afford to do that, but she was shocked. "$25? My parents can't afford that!"

Her friends didn't believe her at first, but she finally convinced them that was out of the question for her family. She was not ashamed to admit it — it was just the plain truth. And truth was honored in the Chisholm family. Candy never lied to her parents, though she was certainly tempted sometimes.

Candy was glad her dad didn't get wind of the planned senior dance, or he might have sacrificed in some way so she could contribute the $25. Her parents always knew money was a necessity, of course, but it was never top priority. That's why Bob worked for peanuts as manager of WONA. He was offered good paying jobs in other towns and cities, but he turned them down because he and Carol felt strongly that it was important for Winona to have truthful news and other things the station provided the community. Besides, they loved Winona.

The irony was that despite his low salary, Bob and Carol were generous beyond their means. Carol was always quietly buying food and other things for people she knew who were struggling financially. She did it discreetly to minimize embarrassment for the recipients — except one time when she took Candy with her, and to this day, Candy deeply regrets the embarrassment it caused her sweet classmate. Candy saw the humiliation in her classmate's face, and understandably the girl never seemed comfortable around Candy ever again.

But other than that one terrible mistake, Bob and Carol both extended dignity to those who weren't getting it elsewhere, friendship to the friendless and had no racial barriers in choosing who to be friends with.

Both of them were very kind people, but Bob's generosity was most often aimed at his wife and daughter. When Candy was maybe 12, some of the girls her age were getting birthstone rings for their birthdays. Their parents would buy them rings with a tiny gemstone. When Candy's birthday was approaching, she told her parents she wanted a ring like the other girls had with a little amethyst stone. Her dad said she would need to prove she was responsible enough for something that valuable, so he gave her a cheap ring from a dime store and said if Candy could take care of it for the two months until her birthday and not lose it, he would buy her a real amethyst ring.

On the day before her birthday, Candy still had the fake jewel, but the cheap plastic band broke in two. She thought she wouldn't get the real ring, but, of course, her dad came through with not just a pretty silver band with a chip-size gem like the other girls had, but a really large square-cut amethyst mounted on a 10-carat gold band with real chip diamonds on either side of the amethyst.

Candy was so proud of that ring, and it is still one of her most treasured possessions.

Bob also showed his generosity when the family travelled once a year to the Mississippi Broadcaster's Association convention, which was always held at high-end hotels in Biloxi along the Gulf of Mexico. Candy remembers sitting down in a fancy restaurant to have dinner with her parents and ordering a hamburger, and her dad said, "A hamburger? Here? Baby, you need to try lobster!"

So she did and loved it, and many years later when she was in Bar Harbor, Maine, with her husband, Bob Willis, and their friends, Suzanne and Chris Sheffield, Candy ate lobster 12 times in 7 days, including lobster pot pie, lobster omelet, lobster salad, lobster bisque, lobster rolls, lobster quiche, lobster with filet mignon and even lobster ice cream. Her daddy would have been so proud!

FLASHBACK: CANDY JUSTICE

When I was a teenager, an old man moved to a tiny rental house on our street. The neighbors understandably avoided him because word had gotten around that he had spent most of his life in Parchman Prison for a murder he committed as a very young man.

But what my mom saw was a lonely old man, who was sick and friendless and was missing an ear. The first day he walked past our house on his way to Piggly Wiggly to buy a few food items, my mother, who was sitting on our porch, hurried down the steps to introduce herself and welcome him to Webster Street.

I think some neighbors thought less of my mother for associating with a criminal, but I was proud of her for being so kind. The man smiled gratefully — probably shocked that a woman would speak to him — and said his name was Mac. She told him to call her Carol, which he never did. My mom and I both always called him Mr. Mac and referred to him that way even when he wasn't around.

Every time Mr. Mac passed our house, if we were outside, Mama and I would speak to him by name.

Then one day, we noticed we had not seen Mr. Mac for a few days. Because we had suspected all along he was nearing the end of his life, Mama made some beef stew and corn bread and took him some. Mama stayed for a while and visited and found out Mr. Mac was indeed dying and either had no family or friends, or none who would claim him. He fully expected to die alone, but was just grateful to not die in prison.

Mama continued to visit and take him food, and then one day she stayed at Mr. Mac's house longer than usual and came home with tears in her eyes, telling Daddy and me that Mr. Mac had just died. She held his hand as he left this world. That day I learned from my mother, without her saying a word, that holding the hand of a dying person is the greatest gift you can give someone.

Spoiled Brat or Miniature Adult

Only-children often fall into one of two categories — the pampered only-child, which is much less common than people think, and the only-child who often has more in common with adults than with other kids.

If you could've seen the Chisholm family's living room on Christmas morning when Candy was growing up, you would've thought she fell solidly into the first category, but in reality, that was the only day of the year she was unabashedly spoiled. The rest of the year, she had to earn and save her money to get a hula hoop or yoyo, just like kids from larger families.

The only child as miniature adult is a far greater reality than the spoiled-brat only-child. In fact, it is so common that parents, if they are wise, have to go out of their way to avoid producing overly precocious, down-right weird kids, who would rather discuss news and world events or math with their parents' adult friends than to play with toys and watch cartoons on TV.

Candy liked a lot of kid pursuits when she was in elementary school, but she was well on her way to being a strange teenager when her mother noticed it and forced her to be normal. Candy's neighborhood friend Elizabeth Hightower announced to some of their friends within earshot of Carol, "Candy won't date any boy who doesn't read the *Wall Street Journal."*

That wasn't true since Candy was too young to date *anybody* and she had never seen the *Wall Street Journal*, much less read it. But Libba's point was well taken by Carol, who told Candy that one day that week, Candy had to invite a school friend, who didn't live in their neighborhood, to come home with her after school to play. Candy said she would be too embarrassed to do that, and her mom said she was going to do it anyway. One of Carol's favorite retorts to Candy saying she didn't want to do something was to tell her daughter gently, but firmly — yes, you will do it, and it will be "good for your character."

So Candy nervously asked a school friend — it was either Kellie Branch or Janie Wilder — to come over and play, and when that went well, Carol told Candy the next step was to invite a *different* school friend to spend the night with her the next weekend. Again, Candy said no, and again her mother said yes. So Candy invited Faye Hood, and both of those acts of bravery were the beginning of several fun, close friendships that went well beyond just talking a bit at school.

While her mother was determined to make Candy a normal kid, she and Bob still talked about grown-up stuff in front of Candy and took her places that most parents don't take their kids. Candy believes that is why she was not then, nor is she now, a person who is easily shocked, which served Candy well after college when she became a newspaper reporter.

Candy having a high tolerance for shock was okay most of the time, but sometimes it badly backfired. Like the time her parents were invited to a Christmas party about 20 miles away in Grenada, Mississippi, at the radio station where several of her parents' friends worked. Bob and Carol took their daughter because they thought it was a family-oriented Christmas party, though it was not, as it turned out. Candy was the only child there.

Her parents never drank alcohol in Winona — Bob because it was illegal to buy or sell alcohol in Montgomery County and he didn't want his enemies to have anything they could legitimately use against him, and Carol refrained because she did not want to be a bad role model for the kids in Methodist Youth Fellowship, of which she was the leader. And the kids really looked up to her and thought she was fun.

In fact, when Candy was a teenager, she sometimes came home and found some of the MYF boys sitting in the wicker rocking chairs there on their front porch asking her mother's advice about something. If it seemed serious, Candy would make some excuse to go across the street to Phyllis Townsend's house and let the MYF boys have their therapy session with her mom.

But Candy's parents weren't in Winona that night of the Christmas party. Still, neither of them had more than one or two cups of spiked punch, and Candy, of course, was given UN-spiked punch. But her dad, who was in a silly mood, picked up the punch bowl and pretended he was drinking the whole batch.

Someone even took a picture. Candy thought that was hilarious, and the next day at school she told her teacher and the other kids about her dad drinking directly out of the punch bowl that contained spiked punch. Predictably, her teacher was shocked, and that night called Carol to complain about their taking their young daughter to a "drunken party."

The next notorious incident happened in Biloxi, Mississippi, at the Mississippi Broadcasters Convention. Because the Chisholms could not often afford a vacation, Bob, Carol and Candy always went to the convention, which was family-friendly and a very fun gathering on the Gulf Coast. And the Chisholms' hotel and other expenses were paid for by the owner of WONA. On the last day of the three-day convention, word spread that the famous blonde bombshell Jayne Mansfield would be singing that night at Gus Stevens nightclub.

Other broadcast couples either weren't interested in going to the nightclub or they had older children who could babysit their younger children back at the hotel. Candy was in junior high school, so her parents took her to see the famous actress and singer perform. And the performance was innocent and fit for someone Candy's age, except for the little matter of an opening act, which turned out to be a non-famous stripper, who started out her act as a fully clothed singer and dancer. When she started flinging her clothes off, Candy was all eyes, and she still wonders how somebody could get tassels to go in opposite circles like that.

Bob and Carol could have gotten up and dragged Candy out of the floorshow when the stripper got down to business, but they didn't — they just looked at each other with facial expressions that said, "We messed up by bringing her here." But they didn't overreact. They didn't sit Candy down and explain that ladies shouldn't take their clothes off in public. They knew Candy already knew that, even though nobody had ever had to tell her.

Thus is the paradox of Candy's childhood and teen years. Both of her parents were very protective of her physically — they took great care to ensure her safety. Therefore, she was not allowed to do some things her friends did because it was deemed too dangerous by her parents, like going to Greenwood or Grenada with another teenager driving.

But Bob and Carol didn't panic if Candy saw or heard something age inappropriate. Was that an only-child thing or just a Bob and Carol thing, where they trusted that Candy wouldn't become a drunken, degenerate axe murderer just because she saw or heard something "scandalous" as a kid?

However, it must be said that Candy was mighty glad her Sunday School teacher Miss Ada didn't get wind of the stripper incident. Miss Ada was a well-intentioned older lady whose heart truly had been broken by not being allowed to be a missionary to China. So she had to be content with straightening out the kids in the Sunday school class.

At Moore Memorial Methodist Church, she ran a tight ship on Sunday mornings with requirements that were of dubious spiritual value, such as making the kids memorize all the names of Old and New Testament books.

They were called on at random to recite the list of books of the Bible, and when they failed to remember them all in the correct order, Miss Ada never told the kids they were going to hell, but she definitely left open that possibility.

When Candy was in mid high school, there was an incident where her being a precocious only-child caused her to act in a way that embarrassed her parents and herself. Ed Forsythe had worked at WONA when he was in college and was now a cherished and very cool family friend. Ed was at the Chisholm house for dinner soon after returning from a trip with friends to San Francisco and wanted to tell Bob, Carol and Candy about it and show them his pictures of the trip.

Before the trip, Ed had just started dating Eleanor "Ellie" Salveson from Greenwood. She was beautiful and charming, and Candy thought she was the perfect dream girl for Ed. In one of his trip photos, Ed happened to be standing next to an attractive woman about his age whom he had met in California. Candy was sophisticated for her age, but not mature enough to know there are some things you just do not say to anybody, even a close friend.

So when Ed said something nice about the young woman in the picture, Candy bristled with jealousy on Ellie's behalf, even though she wasn't there with them. Candy said, "She looks cheap!" Her parents gasped. Candy said she will never ever forget (unfortunately) the look on Ed's face when she made that rude remark. He loved Candy like a little sister, and Ed's face told her she had hurt him deeply by calling his new friend "cheap."

The last thing on earth Candy would have done intentionally was to hurt Ed, whom she adored. Without a formal apology, Ed forgave Candy and went on eventually to marry Ellie. And for the rest of his life, Ed continued to call Candy "Sugar" in his southern gentlemanly accent. Candy learned a valuable lesson that night: *If you can possibly avoid it, never hurt somebody with your actions or words, especially someone you love.*

FLASHBACK: CANDY JUSTICE

When I think of the advantages I have had as an only child, the first thing that comes to mind is that my parents never accidentally left me at a gas station.

Ask any only-child now that they are adults, and they will tell you that one of the good sides of being an only-child is that you are usually close to both parents and get to travel with your mom and dad, because taking one kid on a trip is much more affordable than taking 3 or 4 kids. How about 10 kids? Many years ago, the parents of my friend and colleague Joe Hayden had borrowed a church van to take the whole family, including their 10 children and their Italian grandmother, to visit the Grand Canyon.

They made a gasoline/bathroom stop somewhere in Arizona and were cruising along about 30 or 45 minutes later when Joe's mom did a head count and was horrified that they had left Patrick at the service station.

Joe's dad quickly turned the van around, of course, and when they got back, they found 6-year-old Patrick crying in the arms of the gas station attendant. And 11-year-old Joe and his brothers and sisters got a hearty laugh at Patrick's expense, telling him that they had intentionally left him at the gas station. That couldn't happen in a family like mine with only one child.

THE MEMPHIS YEARS

**Memphis' Beale Street in the 1970s.
Courtesy Special Collections Department, University Libraries,
University of Memphis.**

Chapter 10

That Memphis *Thang*

Never in their lives had the Chisholm family felt such extremes of excitement and dread as they left Winona for a new life in Memphis. They were leaving Winona because Bob had been offered a challenging job as a radio rep, a job that involved radio advertising around the U.S. When he told Carol and Candy about the job offer, they were not enthusiastic.

None of the three of them were ever highly motivated by money, and Carol and Candy did not want to leave their beloved Winona where they were rich in the community's esteem and friendship. Bob had the advantage because he knew he was going to a new job he would like. But Carol and Candy could at first only see what they would be losing.

Years later when we had moved to Memphis, my mother was hired by WDIA, the radio station famous for being the first all-Black programmed radio station in America. She was not on the air, since she was not African American, but she brought much expertise to the behind-the-scenes running of a radio station. She helped establish WDIA's FM daughter station and made life-long friends there and at WDIA, including famous radio and recording personalities like Rufus Thomas and her dear friends, Bob McDowell and Jackie Kelly.

FLASHBACK: BRYAN COTTINGHAM
I met Rufus in 1977 when he was a guest on a television special I was producing in Memphis. He was the first of many stars and

This building contained the offices and recording studio for one of the most important R&B music labels in America in the 1960s and early 1970s. Courtesy Special Collections, University of Memphis Library.

personalities I got to meet and work with as a result of a career that started in Winona. Rufus was as talented and funny in person as he was on the records we listened to in high school. "The Dog" and "Walkin' the Dog," with their wonderful lyrics and slightly naughty dances, were favorites at Friday night post home football game dances at the Winona Community House.

I was having lunch with Rufus one day when the subject of "white" and "colored" restrooms and water fountains in the early south came up.

"Tell me something," he asked me in his gravelly voice. "What color were you when you were born?"

"Well, I guess I was sort of pink."

"And what color do you turn when you get cold?"

"Blue?" I had no idea where this was going."

"And when you get sunburned, you turn red. Right?"

"Yeah."

"And when you die and they put you in the grave, you're gonna turn black. Now look at me. I was born black. When I get cold, I'm black. When I get sunburned, I'm still black. And when they tuck me away in the grave, I'm still gonna be black. And you got the nerve to call ME colored?"

That was Rufus.

··········

Carol couldn't have known that she would soon be working behind the scenes at WDIA, America's first radio station that was programmed entirely for African Americans. WDIA, ironically had a similar place on the radio dial (AM 1070) to WONA (AM 1570).

WDIA, 50,000 watts during the day and 5,000 at night, plays classic R&B music and calls itself "The Heart and Soul of Memphis." The first Black disc jockey in the South was at WDIA, which became known as The Star Maker Station because such famous D.J.'s as B.B. King, Rufus Thomas, Little Milton and Bobby O'Jay got their starts there, and Elvis Presley always said his music was inspired at an early age by WDIA.

Carol Chisholm could call those famous radio people her co-workers once she was hired by WDIA.

When the Chisholm family moved to Memphis, Candy had just completed her freshman year at Ole Miss, and her transition to Memphis was made easier by the fact that some of her friends from Ole Miss were from Memphis, so she had a ready-made set of friends for summers and holidays.

Bob's first Memphis office was at Union and Cooper in Midtown in the building now occupied by Playhouse on the Square.

Candy's first job after graduating from Ole Miss was being a reporter at the Memphis *Press-Scimitar,* also on Union Avenue.

In Memphis, Bob and Carol first lived in an apartment, which they hadn't done since their newlywed days in Montgomery, Alabama. Candy had never lived in an apartment while in college, so her parents' Memphis apartment seemed glamorous to her, especially when they discovered that Stax Records super star Isaac Hayes was their neighbor.

The abundance of everything that big city life offers made life exciting for the Chisholms but when their first Christmas in Memphis rolled around, they felt a huge emptiness when they remembered the warmth of a Winona Christmas.

The Read family, which had lived in Memphis before moving to Winona in the 1960s, called the Chisholms to suggest they meet the Reads at the Memphis airport when they picked up their son, Rick Read, who was a cadet flying in from West Point for the holidays. It was a short but joyous reunion for both families, but when the Reads drove away from the airport to spend Christmas at home in Winona, Carol and Candy's hearts sank, and they wanted to run after the Reads begging, "Take us with you!"

The Brandons and Chisholms
At the Mid-South Fair

Steve and Candy were talking about how much fun their two families had every year at the Mid-South Fair back when the fair used to still be in Memphis at the fairgrounds. Fair food was the biggest attraction for both families. Candy mentioned her dad's devotion to pineapple whip, and Steve went off on a tangent.

"OMG!" recalled Steve Brandon. "Your father and pineapple whip! Your father had a 'system' for attending the Mid-South Fair. First, we had to get ham 'n biscuits from the Boy Scouts (Candy contends it was the Eastern Star booth). Then we walked for a while

Carol at the Mid-South Fair, where Bob and Carol enjoyed junk food every day of the fair's 10-day run. Photo courtesy Candy Chisholm Justice.

until we bought the first pineapple whip. Then roast corn. Maybe some fried pickles. Perhaps a funnel cake. Some fudge. A Frito pie or a corndog with tater tots. Then one more round of pineapple whip. Bob was careful to pace himself so that he could have at least two servings of pineapple whip over the course of the day, maybe three.

"Going to the fair with your folks was always awesome, because Bob's style of grazing his way through the fairgrounds gave me permission, as a kid, to mimic his behavior with impunity. It was always one of the best days of the year!"

FLASHBACK: CANDY JUSTICE

BOB THE PUSHER: When my father was enthusiastic about something, he wanted to spread the joy. This is how Steve Brandon recalled that trait in my dad: "Bob used to get so excited, so energized about stuff. If your father loved something, he unabashedly proselytized about it. I loved that about your dad. One time when we were visiting with your folks in Memphis, and it was time to make lunch plans, your father lit up. 'Hembree, there is this new burger restaurant that will knock your socks off. It serves square hamburgers, straight from the griddle and onto the bun, with the drippings and everything. It's a terrific hamburger, and they make it while you wait. You can also get this delicious soft-serve ice cream for dessert.' That was our introduction to Wendy's. He also introduced us to Danver's and to Grisanti's. Your father ordered my first cocktail for me at Grisanti's on Airways, a Shirley Temple."

Once the Brandons were visiting the Chisholm's in Memphis when Bob offered to introduce them to their new neighbor, a disc jockey who had just started working at WMPS radio.

"This kid is so funny — he's doing things on radio that have

**Bob Chisholm in his new office in Memphis.
Courtesy Candy Chisholm Justice.**

never been done before," explained Bob. "He is a real cut-up, and I wouldn't be surprised if they fire him soon."

So they walked across the parking lot, knocked on the door and that's how the Brandons met Carolyn and Rick Dees. "Your father later arranged for Dees to send a signed copy of the 45, 'Disco Duck,' to me, which sent me over the moon. Your folks were forces of nature."

[Editor's note: "Disco Duck," written and performed by Rick Dees, was one of the last records recorded in Memphis by Memphis artists to go to Number One. It was produced by Stax Records veteran Bobby Manuel, and released on the Fretone label by Estelle Axton, co-founder of the legendary Stax Records].

Bob was right. Rick *did* get fired. And it was because of "Disco

Duck." His career was on the rise, and he had just gotten a lucrative offer to move to rival station WHBQ. Unfortunately, he was still under contract to WMPS and couldn't take the offer. Never one to just sit still, Rick hatched a plan. His station had a strict rule that prevented DJs from playing any record on their program if they had a financial interest in that recording.

"Disco Duck" went on to sell over 6 million copies. Most people would call that a significant financial interest. Rick, as Rick was given to do, played the hit song on his show. The program director immediately fired him, and Rick was free to accept the offer from WHBQ. How would you like to go through the rest of your career being referred to as the PD who fired Rick Dees?

Rick went on to become the most popular DJ in Los Angeles (he was replaced by Ryan Seacrest when he left LA). He had a major role in the movie "La Bamba" and hosted an ABC late night show called "Into the Night Starring Rick Dees." His nationwide "Top 40 Countdown" radio program now earns him tens of million dollars a year.

Chapter 11

Epilogue

Bob had never been athletic or even someone who took leisurely walks to get fresh air, so it was no surprise that as he got into his 60s, Bob's knee joints deteriorated. At first, he coped by getting the management of the building where he worked to reserve a parking space for him next to the elevator. Eventually his knees got so painful that he used a walker to get around and then he had to transition to a wheelchair. Eventually he had to set up an office at home, but he never planned for that to be permanent.

Bob was not embarrassed by his impaired mobility, but he found it frustrating and missed working at the office. He loved work, but also enjoyed spending more time with Carol and Candy, who by then was married with two children and still a full-time reporter at the *Memphis Press-Scimitar*.

Candy often spent Saturday or Sunday afternoon sitting with Bob on his and Carol's porch at their Central Gardens home. Carol had always yearned for them to own a home, but they had never been able to afford to buy a house. It was what Bob wanted to give Carol above all else in the world. As his business prospered, he was finally able to do that. Carol was as thrilled as he hoped she would be about buying a house.

Bob, Carol and Candy all loved the same kind of music — American standards and traditional jazz, especially Jazz vocalists like Carmen McRae and Ella Fitzgerald. Candy enjoyed introducing her dad to the newer jazz vocalists like Diana Krall and Diane Schuur.

On the Saturday or Sunday afternoons that Bob and Candy sat on the Chisholms' porch, they talked a lot but mostly listened to music on a boom box. Candy took delight in scouring local music stores to find a new CD to bring to her dad. She was such a familiar figure in the music stories that the clerks would often greet her with "I've got a great new artist for you and your dad."

One day on the porch, Bob told Candy that he had decided to have knee replacement surgery on both knees. He was tired of being immobile. She had mixed feelings about the announcement. She was so glad for him to regain his health, but was upset when he told her which hospital he was going to for surgery.

Bob and Candy had a big argument about his choice of hospital. Bob had a doctor he liked who only practiced at one hospital. Candy liked the doctor, too, but hated the hospital, where Bob had nearly died a few years before from a ruptured appendix and an infection caused by negligence by the hospital.

When Bob was determined to have his knee surgery at that hospital, Candy, desperate to save her father's life, shouted at him, "This hospital tried to kill you before. Do you want them to have a second chance at killing you? Memphis has plenty of good hospitals but this isn't one of them."

Just before Thanksgiving, Bob went into the hospital and before the surgery, Candy visited her dad, who had asked her to come when her mother was not there. He was afraid Carol would be upset by what he had to say.

Bob told his daughter that he had a lot to tell her and to please listen carefully. He told Candy that if something went wrong and he didn't survive the surgery, Candy would need to take over the business at least temporarily. He said Carol would be grieving and would need Candy to be strong.

Bob talked for a long time about decisions Candy would have to make and who among their clients and associates she could trust and which she could not and many more details. She listened and retained what he said, but she really did not take her dad too seriously because despite the terrible hospital, she, like her dad trusted the doctor. Neither of them knew that the doctor was about to take several weeks off.

Bob came through the surgery just fine, but caught an infection from a nurse, who was forced to work despite being very ill. Bob gradually became very ill and was in and out of intensive care. Candy, who was divorced by then, had to spend most of her time at her newspaper job and home with her young children, but she visited her dad often.

On Christmas morning when Candy's young children were about to open their gifts, Candy answered the phone and the doctor told her to come immediately because Bob might die at any moment. A pulmonologist had been called and Bob was unconscious in intensive care. He died on December 29, 1991. He was buried in Elmwood Cemetery on a cold, rainy day.

Candy wished she had listened more closely to her dad's instructions about how to run his business if he didn't survive his surgery. She never anticipated that she would have to buy a power dress and a few days later get on a plane to go reassure the nice clients and tell off the clients and associates who were trying to take over in Bob's absence.

REFLECTIONS FROM CANDY

My father, Bob Chisholm, died at the age of 62 from complications from "routine" knee replacement surgery. My mother, Carol Burkett Chisholm, lived to be almost 85 and was driving her car and living independently until the last few months of her life. She happily lived and peacefully died in a lovely historic home in Central Gardens in Memphis.

It was the first and only home my parents ever owned. Buying it "for her" a few years before my dad died, was my father's greatest material accomplishment. My son, William Justice, bought the house after Mom died, and he and his two little girls, Sylvia and Roz, live there now. My daughter, Kat Leache, and her husband, Josh Leache and their children Betty and Matthew, live not far away. Mama and Daddy would be pleased that we all live so close to each other.

A couple of years before my dad's death, while he was still healthy, I wrote a long letter to him and my mother recalling special memories of their courage and kindness to many people and thanking them for the many ways they made my childhood and adulthood wonderful. I specified certain ways they had influenced my life.

In the case of my mother, I reminded her of how she used to drive me and several friends to high school football games every Friday night for several years. It was always some combination of Janie Wilder, Faye Hood, Hank Holmes, Robert Herring and me. I don't mean she dropped us off at the home games in Winona. She did that too, but most of all she drove us to away games, and when your team plays in the far-flung Delta Valley Conference, some nights that meant two hours each way.

She would stop for us to all have a fun supper somewhere along the way, and during the trip, she never complained that my friends and I were being loud and silly, though we certainly were. I particularly remember the Friday night after we had first read *Chaucer's Canterbury Tales* in English class. We must have driven my mom crazy with our raucous giggling over the bawdier Chaucer tales. But she never told us to calm down and pipe down.

When we were seniors, I was a cheerleader and could have ridden on the bus with the football players and other cheerleaders, but I much preferred the fun of the Carol Chisholm Football "Bus" with my friends.

One Friday afternoon when we were in the 10th grade, my mom told me apologetically that she was just too tired to make a long drive into the Mississippi Delta that night. I was very disappointed and so were my friends because we all lived for those Friday nights. But nobody complained because we knew we were really lucky to have her so willingly take us on those football trips most Fridays. She deserved a Friday night off, and we knew it.

Nonetheless, after I called the gang and told them the trip was off, I was lying on my bed crying softly. I didn't want Mama to feel bad, so I tried not to let her hear me cry. But she came into my room and sat down on the side of my bed and spoke words I will never forget — grown-up words that I didn't fully comprehend at the time, though I clearly knew those words were very important. Those words and my mom's attitude became the mainstay of my own life when I grew up and became a mother, and they also influenced me as a wife, daughter and friend. My mom's words were spoken tenderly with no sadness, resignation or resentment, no weary sighs and certainly not like a martyr.

"Sweetie, there are so many painful things in life that I will not be able to spare you, but this is one that I can." And then with an excited, happy voice, my mom said, *"Get up and call your friends. We are going to the football game!"*

This from my mom, a life-long baseball fan who didn't even like football. I don't remember the exact things I told my dad in that letter, but I do remember that after he read my letter with tears in his eyes, Daddy apologized to me. "Baby, I didn't do right by you and your mama. I stayed in Winona for 12 years because I loved the station and felt it was important to the people of Winona. But that was a very low paying job, and we never had enough money for me to give Mama a house of our own, a house that was not a rental house. And there were so many things I could have done for both of you financially if I had taken a better paying job somewhere else sooner. I was selfish to stay in Winona."

My answer was in loving sarcasm, if such a thing exists.

"Oh, Daddy, you are *so* right — I would much rather have had some stuff that would have been thrown away by now, rather than a father I could be proud of, a father who made a real difference in the world, a father who would set an example for me as a journalist myself."

He didn't argue, he just smiled and gave me a big hug.

FLASHBACK: BRYAN COTTINGHAM

"Good morning. This is radio station WONA in Winona, Mississippi, with studios in the telephone building."

It was 2008 and the voice of Bob Chisholm once again echoed from the studios of WONA. The station had long ago departed the old telephone building downtown and now sat next to the transmitter on the outskirts of Winona. Bob's voice, recorded on the day the station first went on the air, heralded the beginning of a two-hour celebration of WONA's half century of service to the people of Winona.

I had approached Seth Kent (current co-owner with his wife Sharon) about putting together an anniversary program to mark the

Bryan Cottingham
Photo courtesy Candy Chisholm Justice.

event. He immediately embraced the idea and asked if I would consider producing and hosting the program. I told Seth I would think about it. Like hell I did. I jumped at the chance, just like I had done all those years ago when I was 15 years old, and Bob asked me if I was interested in doing a 5-minute high school news show on the station. Carol and Candy came on board with no hesitation, and we started rounding up old recordings to bring back memories of the early days of WONA.

Former announcer Les Nabors, now a retired Methodist minister, joined us by phone with his reminiscences. We didn't talk about his "short intercourse of music" gaffe, but I did allude to it. Ed demurred with a chuckle and didn't take the bait.

Candy shared the memories of her and her friends having to be quiet while her mother recorded the daily "Mainly for Women" program at home before delivering it to the station for the afternoon broadcast. Carol recalled recording her *Mainly for Women* programs while battling chirping birds outside her window, and how much she admired Bob's hard work and constant dedication to his craft. Both spoke warmly about the many friends they still had in Winona and how much they missed living there.

My main contribution was airing a recording of the embarrassing final moments of my first basketball play-by-play and realizing many of my grandchildren are now older than the squeaky-voiced kid we were listening to on the radio…and that some of them have their own kids.

One of the highlights was when former Piggly Wiggly owner Chut Billingsley stopped by and recreated his famous call-in commercials with me. He even brought in an old newspaper ad from 1958 and used those prices in the commercial.

My old classmate Bob Graves dropped in and recalled his legendary (at least in Winona) call to WLS disc jockey Dick Bionde to report Peanut Holmes' world record clothes dryer tumbling episode.

We all laughed when Bob Graves retold the moment when football public address announcer Fred Watts tipped off Bob and his teammates that their opponent was going to try a fake punt – and that Grenada scored anyway.

The two hours flew by much too quickly. Old friends dropped by the station to say hello and to remember. The local Sonic Drive-in sponsored the program, and when I mentioned on the air how much I loved their limeade drinks, a listener went to Sonic, bought one for me and brought it to the station.

It was a warm reminder of the power of local radio. After the show, several of us gathered at a local restaurant for dinner and more stories. Seth surprised me by giving me the original microphone from the station, the one I had used on my first broadcast. It was, as the introduction to "Twilight Time" promised, "The perfect ending to the perfect day."

THE END

Editor's note: What follows are photos of Memphis' radio legends who impacted not only Memphis with their creativity, but the entire nation. Sam Phillips moved to Memphis in 1945 to work for WREC radio for four years before opening his recording studio and creating in 1952 his Sun Records label that first recorded Elvis Presley. B.B. King worked at WDIA before finding success as a recording artist. Rufus Thomas was an announcer at WDIA before recording his biggest hit, "Walking the Dog." It was to Dewey Phillips, an announcer at WHBQ, that Sam Phillips took Elvis's first record, "That's All Right, Mama." Dewey would later be recognized as America's first "shock jock." George Klein was a radio announcer and TV host, most notably for WHBQ, from the late fifties until the 2000s, when he hosted two Elvis programs on Sirius Radio. A childhood friend of Elvis he was inducted into the Tennessee Radio Hall of Fame in 2013. Rick Dees was an announcer at WMPS and WHBQ in Memphis before recording a hit record and moving to Los Angles to achieve fame at a national level.

**B.B. King in Memphis.
Photo by James L Dickerson**

Sam Phillips
Courtesy Special Collections, University of Memphis Libraries, University of Memphis.

Rufus Thomas
Courtesy Special Collections Department, University Libraries, University of Memphis.

Dewey Phillips, on the right.
Courtesy Special Collections, University of Memphis Libraries,
University of Memphis.

George Klein
Courtesy Special Collections Department, University Libraries, University of Memphis.

Rick Dees in his first TV hosting job on a special produced by Bryan Cottingham. Photo courtesy Bryan Cottingham.

MORE FROM THE AUTHORS

Candy Chisholm

Candy Carries on Bob's Legacy

When I graduated from Ole Miss and got my first journalism job at the *Memphis Press-Scimitar,* I got the good news from Managing Editor Ed Ray, who woke me at 5:30 on a Saturday morning to offer me the job. I did not ask how much it paid and did not bat an eye at the early hour that he was calling. I just wanted the reporter's job, and none of the details mattered to me.

As a born night-owl, I had been very pleased to get a job at an afternoon newspaper. It never occurred to me to wonder why Mr. Ray made his job offer so early in the day. Obviously, he was just an early riser on weekends. I assumed that people working at afternoon newspapers worked in the afternoon and into the evening. Perfect for me!

Mr. Ray told me what day I would start my new job and said that on just that first week, I would start working at 8 a.m. That was really early for me, but I assumed I would shift to a later time soon enough. When I arrived for my first day of work, Mr. Ray told me which desk in the newsroom would be mine and that after my first week, I would always work 5 a.m. until 2 p.m. *Was that a joke or did I just misunderstand him?*

Then he cleared things up for me by telling me that on Saturdays I would start work at 4 a.m. "You mean we work on Saturdays?" I said to myself, not stupid enough to say that to Mr. Ray. Then my sarcastic thought was, "Next, they will be telling me I will be working on Thanksgiving, Christmas and New Year's Eve." Fortunately, I didn't find out that was true until they posted the work schedule for those holidays a few months later. And to add insult to injury, I was assigned to do obituaries on Christmas Day. I went to the ladies room and let myself have a silent little cry in the bathroom stall, getting my act together by the time another female reporter came in. And as it turned out, I did not end up working on Christmas Day because a wonderful colleague, who didn't celebrate Christmas, offered to work in my place.

••••••••

I loved my job, my co-workers and most of my editors. My parents, when they read the newspaper every day, were so proud of me, even when my sole contributions to that day's paper were a bunch of short car wreck stories. Sometimes my stories were so short they didn't even get a byline, but my dad would call me every night at my apartment to find out which stories I had written so he could cut them out, copy them and mail to all his friends.

My first big story to cover was an apartment building fire, in which a woman died, and it happened close to our second deadline of the day at 11 a.m., which was called "the home edition." Our first deadline was for the "star edition" and was at 7 a.m. and the final edition was at 3 p.m. when the stock market in New York closed for the day. The star edition was delivered to outlying towns in our coverage area, the home edition was delivered to the homes of subscribers in Memphis and Shelby County and the final edition went on newsstands around the city.

I was nervous about covering the fatal fire story but didn't realize how much reason I had to be nervous. The fire was out by the time I got to the apartment building, so I began asking the fire fighters for information for my story. They were very helpful, as I would always find fireman to be (in contrast with policemen, who were sometimes hard to deal with.)

I was supposed to get the information, then go to a pay phone (remember, this was 1973) and dictate my story off the top of my head to a rewrite man back at the newsroom, who would type it up as I dictated. He would then rip it out of his manual typewriter and turn it in to the city desk for quick editing, and they would rush it to the composing room on the fourth floor for type setting and from there to the press room on the first floor, where trucks were waiting to distribute the papers hot off the presses.

That's how it was supposed to work, but nobody took the cub reporter Candy Chisholm into consideration. After I asked the firemen my questions about the fire fatality, I rushed to a pay phone and started dictating the story I was "writing" in my head only to have the rewrite man stop me and ask, "How old was the victim?"

To which I replied, "I don't know." To which the rewrite man said, "Go back and ask." So I did, and when I returned to the pay phone and continued to dictate, the rewrite man asked me, "Was the victim alone at the time of the fire?" to which I replied, "I don't know." To which he replied, "Go back and ask." So I did and returned with the answer. Then I dictated more, and the rewrite man asked, "What do the firemen say is the probable cause of the fire?"

To which I replied, "I don't know." To which he replied, "Go back and ask."

It was a very embarrassing start to my journalism career, but what I remember most about that first big story of mine is not the embarrassment, but that the firemen and my newspaper colleagues were amazingly kind and patient with me — well, as patient as you can be while on a crushing deadline.

During my 10 years of working at the *Memphis Press-Scimitar*, I would find that the same personal support and team spirit of that day would characterize my whole time at the newspaper, with a generous dose of laughter and storytelling thrown in. To this day, surviving *Press-Scimitar* people are still extremely close and gather for a reunion every few years or go out for lunch in small groups to reminisce about our time at the paper.

It was exciting and interesting to be a reporter at a big-city newspaper, but in the first six months I worked there, every morning while driving in the dark to work, I felt cold fear that this would be the day they would assign me a story I didn't know how to cover. I thought that day had come when they sent me to cover a plane crash (they don't teach you how to cover those in college journalism classes), but thankfully it turned out to be a false alarm and my inadequacy was not found out. And then one dark morning, I was driving to work, and it suddenly dawned on me that there was nothing I didn't know how to cover.

Sometime during my first year at the *Press-Scimitar*, I experienced for the first time the high of getting a big story when no other reporter in the city was able to. It was the murder of a bank security guard, and police were not letting the press get anywhere near the crime scene, but I was determined and sweet-talked my way past the barricades without lying, which I would never do as a reporter. But maybe blonde hair and a mini-skirt helped a little. I called in my story on deadline, and when I returned to the newsroom, my colleagues applauded me. The assistant city editor Barney DuBois said loudly, "Well, Candy, you finally have printer's ink flowing through your veins."

I was very proud, but I didn't tell anybody that I got the big murder scoop without ever looking down at the dead man lying at my feet.

●●●●●●●●●●

My first eight years at the *Press-Scimitar*, I did a little of everything — covering fires, police, city and county government, trials, writing fun feature stories and even covering fashion in New York for my newspaper. I was married by then and our little girl, Kathryn, had been born. Then on the day I found out I was pregnant with our son William, I was offered the greatly sought-after position of television critic/columnist at our paper. When our city editor Van Pritchartt offered me the job, I told him I would love to accept but I had just found out I was pregnant and he might not want to offer me the position if I would be going on maternity leave in a few months. Van was not usually much of a joker so I thought he was serious when he said, "Well, you can cover TV from your hospital room, can't you — they have TV sets in hospital rooms, don't they?" I was just about to say I would be glad to give birth and immediately start writing my column, but he smiled, and we sealed the deal.

I took a shorter than usual maternity leave, and from home did phone interviews instead of the usual in-person ones. I wrote my daily column, sometimes while holding a crying baby. That led me to many funny and fun conversations with famous people who themselves were pregnant or raising young children and other kinds of conversations with many other TV and movie stars.

My first interview with a TV celebrity was Chuck Connors, who starred in the popular TV series, "The Rifleman." I learned during the phone interview that before he was an actor, Connors was one of only 13 men in American history to play in both the NBA (Boston Celtics) and Major League Baseball (Chicago Cubs and Brooklyn Dodgers). Connors was such a nice man and told me a great story about how he wound up in a barber chair next to movie super star Cary Grant, who humbly introduced himself to Connors. "Hi, Chuck, I'm Cary Grant."

One of my other phone interviews while staying home with baby William was Olivia de Havilland, who was calling from her home in Paris and told me funny stories about the practical jokes they played on the set of "Gone With the Wind." My favorite prank was when they were about to shoot the scene where Rhett Butler has to carry Melanie down the steps during the burning of Atlanta. The rest of the cast asked the wardrobe people to surprise Clark Gable by sewing bricks into de Havilland's hoop skirts. During that interview, deHavilland and I hit it off so well that she would send me a hand-painted Christmas card every year from Paris.

After I went back to work in the newsroom, I was able to travel to LA and New York to cover the TV business. Often I took my husband and children with me, and they went off and did fun things while I worked. But I was having fun, too.

When I had been hired to speak at a university in another part of Tennessee, they insisted that I count up the number of celebrities I had interviewed while a TV critic, and it came to about 500, but only the nicest or nastiest or most boring celebrities stick in my mind after all these years. Most boring: Bob Hope; nicest: Olivia deHavilland; and rudest: Brian Keith, who played the loveable uncle on "Family Affair," but in real life was anything but loveable.

One of my favorites was Jim Nanz, who is still a sports commentator for CBS. Several other TV critics and I had lunch with him in Los Angeles. We were supposed to be interviewing him, but he insisted on interviewing us, enthusiastically asking us fun questions like "What do you think is the best sitcom of all times?" I answered, "The Mary Tyler Moore Show." We reporters and Nanz laughed and talked more than we ate. It was the most fun meal I ever had.

Cybill Shepherd, at the height of her popularity on the TV series "Moonlighting," was at a party on the lawn of a luxury hotel in LA and spotted me across the way. We were not friends, but I had interviewed her once, and we were both from Memphis, so she called me over while she was talking to some of her actor friends.

"Hey, you're from Memphis," she said, "tell these California people what the best donuts in the world are." Without hesitation, of course, I answered, "Krispy Krèmes while still warm," and Cybill started jumping up and down in her evening gown telling her friends, "I told you so!"

It was one of the many fun times when I marveled that I was actually paid to do my job instead of my paying the *Press-Scimitar*.

•••••••••

I have been blessed with three incredible and rewarding careers in my life, all of them revolving around writing—newspaper/magazine writer; teaching college students to write and advising the campus newspaper; and more recently writing mystery novels, (the Britt Faire series), and this my first non-fiction book with my co-author Bryan Cottingham. I am not one of those people who believes writers are born, not made — otherwise I wouldn't have been a writing professor at the University of Memphis for the past 30 years. But I do believe that good writing comes easier to some people than to others and that once writing is in your blood, you have no choice but to write. It's just what you do. And I don't believe you can be a good writer without being an avid reader. The two are inexplicably joined. I would challenge anybody to find a good writer, visit his or her home or office and not find it crammed with hundreds, maybe thousands of books, newspapers and magazines.

•••••••••

After the excitement and fun of being a newspaper reporter and magazine writer — which sometimes involves meeting and interviewing famous people and almost always involves meeting and interviewing *interesting* folks —you might expect the world of higher education to be dull in comparison. But if you think that, you have never worked in a college newspaper's newsroom.

Like any newspaper, a lot of serious work goes on in the newsroom of a college paper. Every day includes digging for news and keeping the public informed, but between deadlines there is no funnier — and at times strange —place. Perhaps that is because there is no better combination than serious young journalists and the exuberance and zaniness of college students.

Nights at the *Helmsman* newsroom have always been especially lively with deadline pressure and the freedom of having the building mostly to ourselves. One of my favorite memories is the time that three *Helmsman* editors—Donna Ogle, Lisa Miller and Renea Leathers—set out for the Tiger Den to pick up some dinner and as they were about to leave the journalism building, they glanced into a classroom where a naked man was standing. They knew immediately he was the notorious man who had been stripping down in various parts of the campus for several weeks.

Instead of screaming or running away, these three tough women were determined to catch the streaker. One editor took off to get the campus police while the other two editors chased the nude man until they caught him, and the police arrested him. They came back to the newsroom, wrote the story and ran it on page one the next day.

Editor Josh Cannon was well known for his ability to do impersonations of everybody from the student government president to faculty members. He was standing in the newsroom one night, his back to the door, doing a spot-on impersonation of one of our faculty members with the rest of us laughing, when who should walk in but said faculty member. The rest of us, who saw what Josh could not see, were trying desperately to get Josh to stop before the faculty member caught on.

In the daytime over the years, between deadlines, the newsroom has often been the site of fun, games and pranks, especially during the time Kimberly Rogers and Danny Linton were on the staff. One day, the chair of the journalism department surprised us by bringing a group from the *Dallas Morning News* to visit our newsroom and found Kim and some other staffers writing racial slurs on the white board. There was an innocent explanation — they were discussing Kim's upcoming three-part series on racism on campus — but the chair and visitors couldn't have known that at the time.

Danny, who was our arts and entertainment editor for 13 semesters during his undergraduate and grad school years, once won a trip to the Oscars because he correctly guessed all the Best Picture nominees. When he returned, Kim and other staffers had come up with a prank to make Danny think a famous movie expert, Roger Ebert, had called and wanted to interview Danny.

Sometimes at the *Helmsman*, an attack came from outside, but the students turned it into a joke on themselves. When editor Michael Paulk accumulated a lot of unpaid parking tickets on campus, he was tried by a student court in absentia and sentenced to pick up trash on campus. The staff and I encouraged Michael to appeal the sentence since it was clearly retribution against the newspaper and an attempt to humiliate Michael for a story the student court didn't like. But Michael very wisely chose to accept his sentence in a good-natured way. And the campus has never been cleaner!

When I think back over 30 years with the *Daily Helmsman,* two incidents that may seem to some to be unremarkable, stand out in my mind. I was driving three students to Jackson, Mississippi, for a conference when we had a flat tire on I 55. It was students Kimberly Rogers, Danny Linton and Amulya Malladi and me, their faculty advisor. We were standing on the side of the highway with no jack. We joked that some Mississippians might not take kindly to us since we looked like a United Nations poster—one Black woman, one Indian woman and two white people. But just as we made that joke, a white man in a beat-up pick-up truck pulled off the highway and offered to help.

Because my Jeep had to have metric tools to do an otherwise simple tire change and my toolbox had been stolen weeks before, that Good Samaritan had to spend hours piecing together tools from the bed of his truck, but finally got my Jeep into a drivable state. His wife, with seemingly no annoyance, had sat in the truck the whole time waiting for him to get our tire fixed. When I offered to pay the man for his help, he would not accept anything and just drove away. Kimberly, Danny, Amulya and I talked about how touched we were by that man's kindness to strangers. Years later, Kimberly said that incident reminded her of our newsroom being wonderfully diverse and how "Nothing was off limits there. We could talk about anything."

The other memory that lingers with me took place one night about 10 years ago. It began sleeting and snowing hard while editor Josh Cannon, managing editor Jonathan Capriel and I were staying late to get the paper out. We had sent the rest of the staff home because of the weather. After the paper was finished and sent to the printer, we went outside and found it very difficult to get our cars cleaned off because the sleet was frozen hard on our windshields, and we had no scrapers, just my one credit card.

Everything was going wrong when I said something the two students thought was out of character for me. We all started laughing and couldn't stop, and when we finally were able to leave for our respective homes, Josh said, "This is a night I will never forget for the rest of my life." Jonathan and I agreed, and so far, the three of us have never forgotten it.

••••••••••

However, it has not always been fun and games. A University of Memphis student once was arrested because federal agents thought he was planning to assassinate the President of the U.S. When he was released, he blamed the *Helmsman* for ruining his reputation, even though we were just one news operation of many who covered the arrest. He threatened me and the reporter who wrote the story, and the journalism department had to get a restraining order to keep the student away from our building.

And in another incident, famous feminist Gloria Steinem spoke out against the *Helmsman* for discriminating against women, even though all our top editors were women, as was the faculty adviser (me). Steinem had no first-hand knowledge about the *Helmsman* but took the word of someone who had a vendetta against our student newspaper. That false accusation haunted the *Helmsman* for six months. It would die down and then raise its ugly and unfair head again. A Native American once accused our staff of stealing his soul because our photographer took a photo of the man in a public place.

••••••••••

When I was hired by the University of Memphis (known then as Memphis State University), it was as a combination of teacher in the Journalism Department and faculty adviser to the student newspaper, *The Daily Helmsman*, which had published continuously since 1931—originally named the *Tiger Rag*.

When I was hired, I was extremely pleased to find out the *Helmsman* is an independent student publication, where the student editors make all content decisions with no interference from the University administration or from me as faculty advisor. As it turned out, sometimes that was strictly true with administrators, but other times it was in name only.

I have worked under four university presidents—V. Lane Rawlins, Shirley Raines, M. David Rudd and now William Hardgrave—and I naively assumed at first that all UofM presidents would be devoted supporters of full First Amendment rights for the Helmsman and its staff. None of them ever publicly said they did not believe student journalists had full First Amendment protections, but some privately fought the Helmsman's court-guaranteed rights time and again. I was *always* on the students' side.

Some presidents during my 30 years at the UofM have supported the *Helmsman*'s rights, even when they did not personally agree with decisions the student editors made. But others have done everything in their power to thwart the student editors, going so far as to cut funding to the Helmsman, threatening and harassing the student editors and threatening to fire me for not trying to get student editors to kill stories that were not advantageous to the University and certain faculty members.

There was one run-in with the University administration that made international news. That attack on the *Daily Helmsman* began in March of 2012 when various administrators tried to keep the student newspaper from reporting on a rape that had occurred on campus. Reporter Michelle Corbet valiantly opposed the administration's attempts to keep the rape story from the public, and eventually the rape report was released and Corbet's story was published.

However, the battle was far from over. In late March, the editors (Casey Hilder was editor-in-chief) learned that another rape had occurred on campus and again administrators tried to keep the rape a secret. The accused rapist was a 23-year-old registered sex offender, who was not a student but who was living in student housing illegally, just yards from two child-care centers. The story by *Helmsman* reporter Christopher Whitten was broken in our student newspaper and already tense relations between administrators and the Helmsman exploded.

When *Helmsman* Managing Editor Chelsea Boozer got involved in the rape coverage, police officers filed a false police report against Boozer and Whitten. When Boozer was on campus interviewing students about the rape, an administrator threatened to have her arrested. There was also talk by administrators of possibly expelling Boozer, who was a model student and was set to graduate first in her class.

In May of that year, I was notified that the University had decided to cut the *Helmsman* budget by $25,000. Letters from alumni and national journalism organizations began to pour into the University president protesting the budget cut, and the situation was even covered by the International edition of USA Today.

Chelsea and I went to the office of the then Dean of Students intending to ask questions about the budget cut, and Chelsea at the last minute turned on the recording device on her phone in her purse, not knowing that the dean would admit that *Helmsman* funding was cut because he and Student Government leaders didn't like the students' choice of stories to cover.

Chelsea and I knew immediately that the dean had committed a First Amendment violation. Recording the conversation without informing the dean is allowable under Tennessee law, so Chelsea and I found a lawyer, Brian Faughnan, who was willing to represent us. He let University officials hear the dean's recorded confession to a First Amendment violation and told them he would be filing a lawsuit in federal court unless the university restored the funding and did a thorough investigation of the situation. The University folded under the threat, and Chelsea graduated first in her class.

As of this writing, I am still the faculty adviser to the *Daily Helmsman* and still teaching writing classes. I love teaching and advising the Helmsman, and most of all I love my students, especially laughing with them and seriously discussing journalistic issues. And if I am fired tomorrow — which can be done without cause, according to Tennessee law — I will still consider it one of the great honors of my life to have trained and supported 30 years worth of young journalists at the University of Memphis, most of whom have gone on to great success.

Raggedy Anns Go National

In many ways, the 1960s was a time of tragedy and struggle, but in the midst of it all, 1967 unexpectedly presented Winona with a chance to smile and laugh and cheer on some hometown girls.

It began in a most inauspicious way as members of the Y-Teens at Winona High School were asked to sign up if they wanted to help provide entertainment for a club party. A dozen or more girls signed up, but when it was time for the one and only rehearsal on the Chisholms' front porch, only eight of them showed up. Later, the no-shows would be very sorry they had missed out on their 15 minutes of fame.

The future TV stars were: Phyllis Townsend, Jo Austin, Pam Harrison, Karla Austin, Peggy Osborn, Jo Ann Hart, Jan Shook and Candy Chisholm. It was really thrown together at the last minute, but they sang and played instruments.

Jan played banjo; Phyllis, baritone ukulele; Karla, bongo drums; Peggy, maracas and Pam, the tambourine. The "instruments" played by the rest of the group were more of the jug-band variety — Jo played a bass made from a washtub, broomstick and piece of rope, which made an amazingly good sound; Jo Ann played a washboard and Candy played spoons borrowed from her mother's drawer of sterling silver flatware.

The students at the club's party got a kick out of the little performance, and the girls thought that was the end of it, but somebody pushed them to enter a local talent contest. So they named themselves The Raggedy Anns and dressed in raggedy clothes instead of trying to look like Raggedy Ann dolls. They finished in third place — prize money $2, which split eight ways came to 25 cents apiece.

Again, they thought that was the end of their show-biz career, but Ed Forsythe had a different idea. He volunteered to be their unpaid manager. The girls thought he was kidding, but this was the drummer in The Downbeats, and he knew something about promoting and booking a youthful musical group. Next thing they knew, they were entertaining the Winona Rotary Club and performing at the Mississippi Farm Bureau Convention.

Ed was not only booking the Anns all over the place, but he was helping them with their repertoire, suggesting songs and arrangements. Jo Ann's big brother, Macy Hart, stopped by one day when they were rehearsing and suggested the Raggedy Anns inject two-part harmony into their songs, and that gave their sound the polish it needed.

Around that time, Ed started dating Eleanor Salveson from nearby Greenwood. The Raggedy Anns thought Ed and Ellie were a dreamy couple and were thrilled when they got married.

·········

The Raggedy Anns' big break came when they won the Montgomery County Fair talent contest, which gave them the right to represent their home county at the Mid-South Fair in Memphis in September of 1967. The Mid-South Fair Youth Talent Contest was a prestigious competition. The winner of that contest won the right to appear on the *Ted Mack Original Amateur Hour* on CBS, a predecessor to American Idol that came along 35 years later.

On the steps of the Winona High School gym, the Anns were sent off by the whole student body cheering them on. They played a few songs and then left for Memphis in a VW van borrowed for them by their manager Ed. He made their reservations at a Holiday Inn in Memphis, and when they arrived that Friday, the girls couldn't believe the marquee at the motel read, "Welcome Mid-South Fair and the Raggedy Anns," again arranged by Ed.

While they were staying there, the Holiday Inn management asked them to perform at the Red Fox Tavern, which they gladly did. Then they headed to the Mid-South Fair to compete in the preliminaries of the youth talent contest. Performing before 1,500 people — they were the last of 39 acts and won the right to return the next Wednesday to compete in the finals.

That Friday night in Memphis took three cheerleaders and one majorette away from the usual football game back home. After the competition, they were having a late dinner at the Holiday Inn, and Bob sneaked off and called United Press International to find out the results of that night's football game. He stood up at dinner and said, "I'll tell you girls about the football game if you promise to be quiet and not alarm the whole restaurant. Winona beat Eupora 19 to 14." Of course, they all shrieked with excitement as only 15 and 16-year-old girls can.

Later, the manager of the Holiday Inn came around and asked if they would stay the next day through lunch to perform for the football fans expected for the Memphis State vs. Ole Miss game. The next day the marquee in front of the motel had been changed to: "At 1 p.m., award-winning The Raggedy Anns."

The Raggedy Anns
Photo courtesy Candy Chisholm Justice.

Considering how tough the competition was at the Mid-South Fair Youth Talent Contest, they were thrilled and surprised that they had won the preliminary and earned the right to return for the finals a few days later. Hembree Brandon, the editor of the *Winona Times,* and Bob Chisholm, representing WONA, both were there in Memphis covering the appearance. In the finals, the Raggedy Anns finished second, which meant they didn't win the appearance on the Ted Mack show, but to their surprise, they were asked to appear on WREG-TV in Memphis and also got a call from the talent scout for the Ted Mack show asking them to audition at the Peabody Hotel. Even though they hadn't won the automatic place on the CBS show since they were only second at the Mid-South Fair, the talent scout wanted them to audition anyhow.

In November, Ed was notified that the Anns had been selected for the Ted Mack show on CBS. Bob's newscast the next day began:

The Raggedy Anns continue their winning ways….and this time it's the big one. The eight-girl singing group from Winona High School was notified last night that they have been selected to appear on nationwide television on the Ted Mack Original Amateur Hour. The show is to be taped Monday night December 18th in the Jackie Gleason Auditorium in Miami Beach, Florida.

Candy sometimes considered her dad to be infuriatingly strict about professional ethics, so it surprised her when he did something very uncharacteristic. In the third paragraph of his newscast, he gave his daughter's name first in the list of eight girls, even though by all rights, the two Austin girls should have been first in the usual alphabetical listing.

After the initial thrill of winning a spot on the Ted Mack show, the reality dawned that the Mack show would not pay for their travel expenses. None of the girls came from wealthy families, so that was a problem since the trip for them and four chaperones (Ed, Ellie, Carol and Phyllis' mom, Betty Townsend) would cost $1,500. Enter Ed, Hembree Brandon, Bob Chisholm, Bobby Baskin, who was president of the Winona Chamber of Commerce, Piggly Wiggly owner Chut Billingsley and Bill Lisenby, manager of the J.A. Olson picture frame factory in Winona. They and others were determined to find a way to send the hometown girls to Miami.

The Chamber sponsored a Raggedy Anns Talent Show featuring them and other local talent. All proceeds would go toward the trip to Miami. The J.A. Olson Company offered to pay for all their plane tickets ($80 round trip for each girl).

On December 16, 1967, there was a going away party for the group and their parents at Raggedy Ann Jo Ann's house hosted by her parents Reva and Ellis Hart. They left for Memphis at 10 p.m. Candy had on a pretty suit her mother had sewn and wore a white carnation corsage her dad bought for her. Several of the girls carried Raggedy Ann dolls with them. For most of them, including Carol and Betty, it was their first time on an airplane. At the Memphis airport, they were thrilled to find that their fellow passengers included Sam the Sham and the Pharaohs, a popular rock group at the time.

In Miami, their hotel was the Biscayne Terrace Hotel ($10 a day for double occupancy). Their first night there, the Raggedy Anns had no rehearsal or other duties, so Ed decided the girls and chaperones should go out for a nice dinner at an Italian restaurant. Ed and Ellie went ahead of the others to make sure enough tables were reserved.

The others were to come in two taxis. The first taxi, with chaperone Carol Chisholm and four of the Raggedy Anns, arrived on time at Pichola's Italian Restaurant. The second group with chaperone Betty Townsend and the other four girls arrived and were suddenly aware that something had gone terribly wrong.

Was it a language problem caused by a car full of people with Southern accents and a cab driver from another country? Instead of arriving at the fabulous Pichola's restaurant, they were at the similarly named strip joint, Picallo's.

The cab driver was determined to unload Betty and her charges in a sketchy neighborhood at a dark building with a neon sign flashing the word "DANCERS! While Betty was trying to get the situation sorted out with the driver and his dispatcher, 15-year-old Jo Ann Hart was repeatedly begging her chaperone, "But Mrs. Townsend, we're here, can't we just go in and look for a minute?!

****

The girls had been told by the production supervisor for the Ted Mack show to leave their raggedy polka dot costumes at home and to dress in nicer clothes for the show. And they told the girls to slow down the tempo of their number, "Gonna Get Along Without You Now." The Anns had rehearsal all day on December 18 and taping from 8:30 to 9:30 that night with a studio audience at the Jackie Gleason Auditorium.

Before they left on December 19, they had time to go to the beach (a thrill for Mississippi girls who had never experienced a hot December) and roam around Miami. They stumbled upon actor Dennis Weaver, who was taping a scene for his TV show *Gentle Ben* on a Miami street.

When he heard the Raggedy Anns' Southern accents, Weaver, with a friendly smile, asked them in a folksy drawl, "What y'all doin' in Miami? Just actin' a fool?" The girls had to admit that was exactly what they were doing.

FLASHBACK: CANDY JUSTICE

Thirty-seven years later — when the Raggedy Anns were all in their 50s, had careers and our own families — six of the eight of us walked into the performance venue of the Winona performing arts group Hill Fire, still not sure this was real and not just a far-fetched dream. Hill Fire had decided to pay homage to that year when nearly everybody in Winona was excited about the meteoric rise of the hometown girls, who had grabbed their 15 minutes of fame on nationwide TV.

It was surreal for us middle-aged Raggedy Anns to sit in the audience and watch ourselves depicted by seven cute high school girls who even sang some of our signature songs.

Ed and Ellie's romance played a significant role in the script. And WONA and my late dad's recorded voice made a cameo appearance as well. Some of us Raggedy Anns had tried over the years to find a video tape of our Ted Mack appearance. I even went to a CBS TV archive in New York City, but no luck.

We had given up on ever seeing our TV appearance again. But our dear high school friend Frank Wall was apparently more determined than we were. Or more resourceful (both actually) and he tracked down the Ted Mack episode at the Library of Congress and spent a considerable amount of his own money to get a copy.

Even though we Raggedy Anns knew our appearance on the Ted Mack show would be depicted in the Hill Fire play, we never dreamed that the real thing would be shown on stage during the play's climax. Frank and Hill Fire's Paula McCaulla had kept that from us, wanting us to be surprised. We Raggedy Anns all gasped and hugged each other, not believing our eyes as the video was shown during the play. And speaking of eyes, tears were flowing from ours.

Not long before the show had started, someone in Hill Fire said they wanted us to sing one of our numbers at intermission. First we laughed, thinking they were joking. Then we panicked and said no. We had not sung together in 37 years, but it was a night for being good sports, so we sang one song and surprised ourselves by *not* sounding terrible.

And even if we had sounded terrible, we could see in the faces of the audience of old friends, former classmates, former teachers and folks who had heard *about* but never *actually heard* the Raggedy Anns — that they were not seeing middle-aged has-beens but rather the girls we had once been. And as we sang for the crowd, sitting right next to us were our beloved Ed and Ellie Forsythe, holding onto each other and smiling proudly at us, their girls.

Candy's Greatest Inspiration — or Was She?

Most of my life, I would have said I was inspired to become a journalist by Bessie Ford, a woman I only met once but who left a lasting impression on me. From childhood through my college years, I always attended with my parents the Mississippi Broadcasters' Convention, which met every spring in Biloxi.

At the convention hotel, there was always a hospitality suite set up where MBA members and various MBA guests could have a drink and mingle. I was too young to drink and didn't have any interest in hanging out with my parents' friends, so I was surprised when my dad said there was somebody in the hospitality suite that I would enjoy meeting.

He escorted me into the suite, where my eyes and ears were immediately riveted on a woman, who was holding court, as they say, telling exciting and funny stories about covering Alabama Governor George Wallace and other well-known politicians.

Because the woman was the center of attention, I assumed for some reason that she was considerably older than I was, only finding out last fall from her obituary that she was just nine years older than I. She died at the age of 80 after a very distinguished career in journalism, according to her obit.

I hung on her every word that night in the hospitality suite and when I left her presence, I knew exactly what I wanted to do professionally. It is surprising that I didn't keep up with her accomplishments at all. In fact, I don't think I ever heard her name again. Probably because her most famous reporting was done in Alabama.

And yet as I read her obituary recently, I discovered our paths almost crossed many times. She was the United Press International wire service reporter and bureau chief in Montgomery, Alabama, where I was born.

I was a journalism major at Ole Miss, where she had been a journalism major a few years before me. After college, she had worked for a while at UPI's Memphis bureau, which had its offices in a room just off the newsroom of the Memphis Press-Scimitar, where I later worked as a reporter and editor for 10 years and I knew well the UPI reporter who followed her in the job.

I found out from her obit that Bessie Ford was an only child, like me. My experience all my life has been that only children are drawn to each other.

In her obituary, people who had worked with her over the years described her as a "hard-nosed newsperson" with sources within the state governments of Mississippi and Alabama that other members of the press corps "would give their right arms for." Others described Bessie as "steadfast" and "independent" and one of her colleagues said she was "an honest observer and reporter." After her death, Bessie Ford was described as "a force in the political era of her time."

Bessie Ford had a long, exciting life and didn't need my tribute to her. Yet, when I found out she had died so recently, it made me sad that I had not made some effort over the years to thank her for her inspiration and influence that night in the hospitality suite of the Edgewater Gulf Hotel — inspiration that led me to the most wonderful career I could ever have.

And yet, as I co-wrote this book with Bryan Cottingham, who always considered my dad to be his mentor, I gradually became aware that the actual greatest professional inspiration of my life was not wonderful Bessie Ford, but rather was my own father, Bob Chisholm, who taught me with his actions and attitudes — sound reporting techniques; journalistic ethics; news judgment; to abide by the same high standards you hold others to; to avoid conflicts of interest; how to show compassion for those who may be adversely affected by your reporting and yet still report the news accurately, boldly and fairly; and how to give voice to the voiceless.

These are tenants of the Society of Professional Journalists, but they were also the tenants of my dad's daily life as a newsman, and he was the best teacher of all.

And Daddy, just want to let you know, if you are listening, that I did forgive you for sending me roses to my desk in the newsroom on my first day as a professional, ruining my attempts to seem like a tough reporter. I'm glad you never knew that I hid the vase of roses under my desk.

One of Candy's first radio promotions.
Photo courtesy Candy Chisholm Justice.

Bryan Cottingham   Photo courtesy Seth Randles.

Bryan Continues Bob's Legacy
What's a Kid from Winona Doing in a Place Like This?

A lot has happened since my last broadcast on WONA. Coming out of high school in 1964, I was set to go to Ole Miss on a full scholarship. That all changed when my family moved to Memphis a few months after graduation, and I discovered Memphis State University was introducing one of the first Radio/Television majors in the country. That was a no-brainer. Forget the scholarship. Here was my chance to go to college AND study my dream. It didn't hurt that tuition was $72.50 a semester and I could live at home.

Two weeks later I joined 15 other students, all with a background similar to mine, as freshmen sharing a common dream. We were the first college Radio/Television majors in the southeast. Our professor, David Yellin, had been a writer on the original Superman radio series and seemed to know everyone.

I remember dinner with Fred Friendly, the producer behind Edward R. Murrow's "See it Now" broadcasts and later president of CBS news. I was awe struck as he described behind-the-scenes stories about the infamous radio broadcast that brought down rogue Senator Joe McCarthy.

Late in my freshmen year, my fellow students and I built the campus radio station and started broadcasting by phone wires to the dorms. Early audiences were sparse to say the least, but we didn't care. We aired our programs as if the million listeners we imagined were real. Youthful naiveté and enthusiasm overcame any thoughts we might not always know what we were doing. We learned from effort, not just from reading.

Bob Chisholm's early lessons about work ethic and integrity stuck with me and I always approached student projects as if they were happening in the real world. Sometimes they did. Local radio stations sometimes aired our projects. On Sunday nights, rock legend WMPS aired news from local colleges on Classroom 68, a three-hour version of the WONA high school news program that started my career. One night, I interviewed a Memphis State student who was working his way through college as a magician. I even had him perform a couple of magic tricks on the radio while I described them to the audience. His real name was James Will Surprise (his father, John Will Surprise, Jr., was a Major Surprise in the Air Force). Jim became a lawyer and was my closest friend for 42 years until his death in 2006. But I digress.

In 1965, before computers, college class registration was an all-day ordeal involving standing in line for hours and then often discovering the course section you wanted was full. This meant finding another class time, often causing a conflict with some other class you were taking and forcing you to revamp your entire schedule. Using my WONA experiences with county and statewide election coverage, I set up a closed-circuit operation that officials later said cut registration time by 30 percent more.

Student volunteers put up a system of loudspeakers at strategic points around the gymnasium where registration took place. We played music to entertain the students in line, but our main objective was information. I stationed several reporters and runners inside the gym to gather and pass on critical information about class closings, including warnings about which classes were beginning to fill up. This allowed students to re-plan their schedules without having to wait and do it inside. This was the biggest and most welcome time saver. We also aired reminders about procedures, required documentation and tuition and fee payments. Live interviews with the college president, bursar, department chairs and students who had been through the process rounded out the day. One of the extra benefits was the chance for my crew and me to pre-register a day early since we would be busy on registration day. I also got an A for the semester in a three-hour self-directed project course that started and finished on registration day. Bob had taught me to be resourceful.

When I was a junior, the real world stepped in. I applied for a booth announcer's job (off camera) at the local Public Television station. I was disappointed to find out the job had just been filled but was elated when I was offered a job as master control operator. I quickly said yes (I was newly married) and then asked what a master control operator did.

The chief engineer laughed and explained I would be directing station breaks between programs, loading and airing film and slide promotions and loading and setting up film and videotape programs. In 1967 there was no PBS (Public Broadcasting System) network. NET (National Education Television) was a series of non-connected local television stations that aired film and videotaped programs that were bicycled (mailed) from one station to another.

For a year and a half, I learned how television worked – and loved every minute. I watched the directors put together their programs and was intrigued. I thought, "I can do that" (and I believed it). This reminds me what Bob said years later when he introduced me to a colleague. "One of the things I always liked about Bryan," he said, "is that he was always willing to try anything new." Then he chuckled and added, "And I always felt he thought he could do it better than anyone else." This is probably why my wife once referred to me as a "Cocky Little S***" and had a shirt made for me with the monogram *CLS*. I blame Bob. He always encouraged me to try new things, and to do them better than I could. And he always supported me.

The next stop was WMC-TV, the NBC affiliate we used to watch in Winona. For the next 12 years I was given chance after chance to try new things, make new mistakes, learn new skills and move up the ladder. Starting with my first live program, Romper Room, I produced and directed over 5,000 programs and specials, ranging from news and public affairs, studio wrestling with Jerry "The King" Lawler, election coverage, special events, sports and myriad specials, including coverage of Elvis Presley's death and funeral.

"Elvis just came into the emergency room, and I think he's dead." This hurried call from the wife of one of our news photographers, an ER nurse at Baptist hospital, set off a frenzy of activity at the station that did not end until his burial three days later. It was also the beginning of over 75 hours without sleep for me. As the newsroom hurriedly dispatched reporters, cameramen and news vans, I took charge of the production of what I knew would be a constant stream of reports, updates and ever-changing priorities. Since reporters were already leaving the station, I went upstairs to the announcer's booth as we interrupted our regular program.

Over a simple "Bulletin" slide I told viewers, "We interrupt our program for this special report from Action News 5. Elvis Presley has been taken by ambulance to Baptist hospital where doctors are now working to save the life of the 42-year-old entertainer. Stay tuned to WMC-TV for further news as it happens." It was a short and simple announcement that was the first to alert the world of what soon became devastating news.

Bryan with Today Show host Hugh Downs, directing a special edition to be broadcast from Memphis. Photo courtesy Bryan Cottingham.

Ten minutes later, I was sitting at the control room panel when I switched to a live shot outside Baptist Hospital where reporter Mason Granger calmly, but gravely, announced, "Elvis Presley is dead." He went on to give the sketchy details we knew. At that moment, WMC-TV abandoned all local and network programming.

The next three days were devoted to around-the-clock coverage of one of the biggest events of my broadcast career. Anchored by our studio news team, we shifted from live reports to interviews, biographical information, condolences, logistical details and world reaction. At several points I did live reports for radio and TV stations around the country and in parts of the world that had just gotten the news. I coordinated network coverage for the correspondents and crews that had flown into Memphis for the shocking event. At 2 a.m. I led an NBC network crew to Memphis International Airport to cover the arrival of Priscilla Presley aboard Elvis' private Jet, "Lisa Marie."

WMC had the only live remote capability in Memphis, so much of the coverage I produced was seen around the world as it happened. Remote coverage is taken for granted today, but in 1977 the technology was much more primitive. We dispatched a helicopter to circle Graceland (and later to cover the funeral procession) and broadcast live pictures, an unheard-of capability at the time. A news photographer sat next to an engineer who was holding a microwave dish.

Both were strapped in but had their feet dangling over the side of the helicopter. The engineer held a microwave dish pointed at the ENG (Electronic News Gathering) van 500 feet below as the chopper circled above Graceland. The signal was processed in the van and routed to the control room back at the station for broadcast.

Reporters interviewed celebrities and fans, over 100,000 of

whom had turned out.

Coverage continued uninterrupted by commercials or regular programming until the end of the funeral. Near the end of the ceremony, I was still trying to figure how to end our coverage appropriately. Then an idea hit. I dispatched a production assistant to the WMC-FM radio station across the hall from us and told her to bring back Elvis's Gospel album, "His Hand in Mine," the album that had won his only Grammy Award.

As mourners reluctantly departed the cemetery, we played his version of "In My Father's House are Many Mansions." The reporters went silent as the world said goodbye for the last time. Our coverage was over. I drove home and fell in bed, but only after telling my 9-year-old son "Happy Birthday" and apologizing for missing his party the day Elvis died.

My time at Channel 5 had some early Winona connections. When I was in the fifth grade, some of my classmates made the two-hour trip to Memphis to sing and dance on "Talent Showcase," a Saturday morning live program featuring youthful performers. We were all impressed to watch The Suzettes, Claire Allen, Penelope Harrison, Sharon Hales and Kay Oliver sing and dance on live TV. Twenty years later, I was assigned to produce and direct that program. By then, the Suzettes were a little too old for an encore performance.

A couple of years after that, we started airing Quiz 'Em on the Air, a weekly high school competition that featured panelists from two area high schools as they answered current event questions taken from the pages of the *Commercial Appeal,* a Memphis morning paper that had circulation down as far as Winona. In 1963, I had been a part of the Winona High School team, along with Barbara Bryan, Sharon Hales, Patricia Perrin, Thomas Garrett and

Martha Curtis. Our history teacher, Fonnie Mae Furness, was our coach and prepared us beautifully. We only missed a total of two questions in five matches and won the Mississippi state championship. You guessed it. Ten years later, I got the nod to produce and direct the program in Memphis. It even featured the same *Commercial Appeal* editor who had been the judge the year we won.

By far, my greatest enjoyment at Channel 5 came during the years I spent directing Studio Wrestling. It was the most popular television program on Memphis television. Every Saturday morning, the baby faces and the heels (the good guys and the bad guys) faced off in our studio, determined to fight, maneuver and cheat their way to victory. It was controlled (most of the time) chaos and I was happily in the middle of it.

When the program first came to WMC-TV, promoter Jerry Jarrett asked me how much I wanted to know. I told him I didn't want to know what was going to happen. I just wanted a few hints so I would not get caught off guard and miss something. Otherwise, I might anticipate something and give away the ending.

A good example was the time Jerry "The King" Lawler told me before the program that I needed to make sure his Cadillac stayed in the shot all the time during rival Bill Dundee's interview. Bill had "won" the car from Lawler the week before and was going to have it in the studio with him as he vowed not to give the King a chance to win the car back in a rematch. Dundee played the interview for everything he could. He cried as he talked about growing up as a poor lad in Australia and how he always dreamed of having a Cadillac. Now his dream had come true.

I was even getting a little misty eyed when Lawler suddenly burst through the studio door wielding a baseball bat. He ran to the car, and just a few feet away from the "astonished" Dundee, smashed the windshield twice with his bat, all the while screaming at Dundee and demanding a rematch. Through his tears, the diminutive Australian angrily agreed to a championship match the following Monday…and promptly "lost" the car back to Lawler. It was *Hamlet,* without the melancholy soliloquies. It was the moment that inspired my slogan, "Life is fake. Television and pro wrestling are real." A plaque with that sentiment sits on the shelf of a bookcase right behind me in my home office today.

The *Hamlet* analogy also gave me another idea. I took a crew to the Mid-South Coliseum to film the live matches. I then edited the footage to fit quotations from Shakespeare, such as a recitation of "Double double, toil and trouble" from *Macbeth* as two heels double-teamed a young baby face to cheat their way to victory. "Shakespeare Goes to the Matches" produced one hilarious moment during the editing.

Randy Paar, the daughter of early *Tonight Show* host Jack Paar, was working with me on the project. She had just come to work at the station, and we had become good friends. As we listened to a recording of Richard Burton's *Hamlet* to find a particular speech, Randy started laughing. "I remember Richard coming to our house for dinner one night," she explained. "After we ate, he got drunk and stood on a coffee table in the den as he recited the entire second act of *Hamlet*, playing all the parts." And I thought MY childhood was interesting.

A few years later, I directed a national Pay-Per-View wrestling special in Chicago. The program featured a series of matches pitting stars from the Memphis region against those in the Texas region. These were considered to be the two best wrestling territories in the country. The main event matched Jerry Lawler against the Texas champion in a 60-minute no disqualification contest. It was an hour-long bloodbath as one wrestler and then another gained the advantage over his opponent. Neither was able to pin the other, and after time expired, both men were carried from the ring on stretchers, unconscious and covered with blood. An hour later, I was having dinner with the King at our hotel. A band-aid on his forehead was the only evidence of the gory ordeal. Yep, life is fake. Television and pro wrestling are real.

After almost 14 years of local broadcasting, I decided it was time to move on, and hopefully, upward. I spent a year and a half at a local advertising agency where I got experience directing high budget commercials and corporate programs. During that time, I once again made use of my experiences with Bob Chisholm and WONA, this time to enter the political arena. Bob had introduced me to politics. From his coverage of local officials and proceedings to his political activism, he taught me by example.

The ad agency was owned by a man who had run successful statewide campaigns for several senators and governors. As director of broadcast production, I wrote, produced and directed commercials for two congressmen and two governors. I was also the communications director for their campaigns, and later served as an advisor after they were elected.

I was lucky. Politics was not as nasty and polarized as it is today. Both governors, Joe Frank Harris of Georgia and Fob James of Alabama, were good men who also became friends. I loved sharing political stories and strategies with Bob during that time.

Bob Chisholm taught me not to be afraid to attempt new things. He was constantly giving me new responsibilities and duties, always with good direction and the freedom to grow and to make mistakes and learn. Armed with that philosophy and tempered by 21 years of

Top: Bryan, center, with Mickey Gilley at a planning session.
Photos courtesy Bryan Cottingham.
Bottom: Bryan giving direction to Jerry Reed.

radio, television and advertising agency experience, I quit my job at the age of 36, sold our house, packed up four kids and a wife, who was eight months pregnant, and moved to Nashville without a job. It was time to go out on my own. I made $300 in the first three months. Did I mention the term CLS? Maybe the C stands for Crazy.

I trudged through the streets of Nashville week after week, returning home each night discouraged but not beaten. With only about three weeks of money left, the newly formed Nashville Network (TNN) called me back and offered me a job.

Two days later, I heard from WSM-TV, the leading station in Nashville and probably the number one television in the Midsouth. They also wanted me to come to work for them. The jobs were good, but I was determined to work for myself. I hadn't risked everything just to take a small step upward.

I called Bob, not for advice, but for confirmation I was doing the right thing. He encouraged me to follow my instincts and reminded me of my talents. I took a deep breath and turned down the security of both jobs, buoyed by Bob's observation that these offers verified my abilities and proved I was marketable. I was convinced I was doing the right thing, even though some people probably thought I was crazy.

I remember golfer Lee Trevino once responding to a reporter's question about the pressure of facing a long putt to win a $1,000,000 tournament. "That's not pressure," he explained. "Pressure is facing a five-foot putt to win or lose a $25 bet when you only have three dollars in your pocket."

I was facing a 50-foot putt with $600 in my pocket, no job, a wife, five kids and rent that was due in three weeks. I putted, closed my eyes and waited for the sound of the ball dropping into the cup. A week later, I heard the beautiful thud of a golf ball finding its target. I was sitting in yet another outer office waiting for yet another interview when I picked up a newspaper to pass the time. As I thumbed through the pages, I saw a small article buried on page 13B. A small headline whispered, and then screamed to me, "Local Start-Up Company to Broadcast National Pay-Per-View Football and Basketball Games."

As soon as I got home from the interview, ("You have great credentials, but we just don't have any project at the moment that requires your expertise.") I searched for the phone number of this impending miracle.

I dialed the telephone and asked to speak to the president. Why waste time with the people who can only tell you "maybe," when you can just go right to the person who can tell you "yes"? He answered. We talked. I asked. He said yes. The dam broke and my career suddenly cascaded onward and upward.

The next 40 years have been filled with adventures, challenges and opportunities that have taken me to New York, Hollywood, Las Vegas, Washington, D.C., offshore oil rigs, iconic football and basketball stadiums, exotic locations, river barges and four prisons around the country. Along the way, I have worked with and gotten to know celebrities, stars, politicians, CEOs, sports figures and fascinating people I had never heard of.

FLASHBACK: BRYAN COTTINGHAM

After I moved from Winona to Memphis, Hembree occasionally made references about my career in his *Winona Times* column. Around 1972 he called and asked if I could get Steve and Lisa on the very popular "Magicland" program I was producing and directing. Of course. That was an easy way to repay the guidance and support from Hembree when I was starting out.

The family came to Memphis for the taping and Hembree sat with me in the control room while I directed the show. I noticed he was taking notes and shooting pictures during the program, but I didn't think much about it.

The following week I got a call from my aunt in Winona.

"Have you seen this week's *Winona Times*? You're in it."

I told her Hembree had been to Memphis for the taping and that he usually made a small mention in his column when we had talked or seen each other. "Bryan, it's a full-page story!" I was shocked. Hembree had written a "Winona Boy Makes Good" feature, complete with pictures. It was flattering and a bit overwhelming, and it speaks to the impact of media attention in a small town.

The Lone Ranger Rides Again

About 15 years ago, I was feeling nostalgic and Googled, "The Lone Ranger. "As I listened to the opening, I started wondering if Fred Foy, the golden voice who invited listeners to return to those thrilling days of yesteryear, was still around. I searched a little more and found a Frederick W. Foy who was living in Woburn, Massachusetts. The letter I later wrote to Fred's widow after Fred's death explains what happened next:

> I was very saddened to hear about your husband's death. He was one of the giants of early radio and continued as one of the great voices ever to grace the airways. Beyond his talent, however, I was fortunate to have gotten to know him in the last three years and to discover his talent was surpassed by his kind and generous nature.
>
> Like so many baby-boomers, I grew up listening to the radio and being thrilled every time I heard the opening strains to the William Tell Overture, followed by that golden voice imploring me to "Return with us now to those thrilling days of

yesteryear." To this day it remains as the greatest opening to any radio or television program ever. As a five-year-old boy, I discovered the amazing effect that a voice, wielded as a slashing saber or woven with the delicacy of an epee, could generate.

Without my knowing it at the time, that moment planted the seed that later bloomed into a 50-year career in radio and television. About three years ago I decided to search the Internet to see if I could find a recording of the original opening to the Lone Ranger radio show. The moment I heard the music, along with Fred's inimitable voice, I felt a chill as I was immediately transported back to my family living room and found myself listening breathlessly as another early frontier adventure unfolded.

Although most of my career has been in television, my favorite times have been spent in radio. From the time I started as a 15-year-old DJ in a small town in Mississippi to the voice-over work to the oldies radio shows I did later in my career, I have always remembered the lessons I learned listening to Fred. A voice is an instrument to be played with grace and dignity, with fervor and passion and used with unbridled joy to evoke responses and emotions from those who listen. It is a rare gift from God, never used more lovingly than by Fred Foy. I will miss his voice and the brilliant way he used it to tell a story and elicit feelings.

I am thankful that I had even a brief opportunity to share his warmth and his generosity as he made a 61-year-old kid feel young and special again. I know you and your family will miss him. You are all in my prayers as you deal with your loss. Your remembrances of him will go well beyond the memories of the countless millions he touched with his voice. But to each of us, our memories of him are very special.

The autographed photo of himself Fred Foy sent to Bryan Cottingham
Photo courtesy of Bryan Cottingham.

FLASHBACK: BRYAN COTTINGHAM

The moment inspired me to search further to find out more about Fred. My last recollection was hearing him on the Dick Cavett Show, so I started my search there. When his bio showed he was living in Woburn, I decided to make a bold move.

In all my years as a television producer/director/writer, I have worked with a number of celebrities. Never once in that time have I ever asked for an autograph or written a fan letter, but I decided that I needed to tell Fred how much influence he had exerted on my life and what an inspiration he had been to me.

When I called, I got his voice mail. I didn't have to hear him say his name to know that this was indeed the voice that had thrilled me so many years before. I decided not to leave a message but waited instead to call back the next morning. When Fred answered the phone, I felt like a kid again. I haltingly explained the reason for my call and stumbled some as I told him he was the reason I had gotten into radio and television.

He thanked me for my call and immediately put me at ease when he told me I had made his day by calling him. All of a sudden, it was as if we were old friends. He told me stories about how he had gotten into radio and regaled me with behind-the-scenes anecdotes about the Lone Ranger.

Before I knew it, 45 minutes had gone by, and Fred was asking for my address. He sent me an autographed picture that now sits in a frame atop a classic old radio I have in my home office. He also sent a copy of his book and his taped reminiscences. Later in the year I got a nice Christmas card from him in which he once again thanked me for my call.

I can sum it up this way, "Fred Foy was my early hero. Bob Chisholm was my mentor, my inspiration and my friend.

FLASHBACK: BRYAN COTTINGHAM

Once again, my time at WONA and my later career converged. Around 1990 I directed an awards show that originated in the Jackie Gleason Auditorium in Miami, whose stage had been graced many years before by the Raggedy Anns.

Our production office was in the old rehearsal hall used by the June Taylor Dancers. There was a big white circle painted in the middle of the floor. This was used by the dancers to rehearse the high angle shot in every opening routine that showed the dancers making a circular pattern and moving their arms and legs in and out of the circle. A few years later, I used the television remote truck that served as the control room for the Gleason show. The TeleMundo truck was my control center for producing and directing some college basketball games.

All the while marveling, "What's a kid from Winona doing in a place like this?"

When I retired, I realized there was still more I wanted to do. Bob had always been so generous to me with his time and his encouragement. I wanted to repay this kindness. During my career I had tried to follow his example by mentoring young people who came into the business with the same passion I had. Retirement was my chance to give back more.

When I was 65, I returned to college to finish the bachelor's degree I had abandoned so many years before. It was interesting to be in the classroom where I was older than all my classmates…and all my teachers. In one history class, we were discussing America's involvement in the space race, particularly the landing of an American on the moon. The teacher's PowerPoint presentation included a picture of President Kennedy addressing Congress in May of 1961 as he challenged the country to meet the goal of, "Landing a man on the moon and returning him safely before the end of the decade."

I raised my hand and asked if I could show her something. I picked up a yardstick and walked to the screen. "Do you see the group of Congressmen up here in the corner," I asked. "That short person standing with them is me." I was a 14-year-old Congressional Page at the time. In fact, I opened the door for the president to come onto the floor of the House of Representatives to give this speech. What a thrill for the kid from Winona.

I soon walked across the stage to receive my college diploma, only 50 years after I had started. A year and a half later, I had my master's degree safely clasped in my hand. My wife (much younger than I am) posted a picture of me in my cap and gown on Facebook with a congratulatory message and the comment, "Now I can go somewhere without having to explain that my 68-year-old husband couldn't be there with me because he had to do his homework." I could devote another entire book to my life with Julie. But, again, I digress.

For the past 10 years, including some of the time I was in school, I have been tutoring grammar and writing and teaching communications at Nashville area colleges. I love the interaction with students and I learn so much from them. Every time I see a young person respond to what I am teaching, every time I get an e-mail or a comment thanking me for what they have learned, I think back to that time over 60 years ago, when a man with the gifts of integrity and caring and the enormous desire to share those gifts, put his arm around the shoulder of a 12-year-old boy and said by his every action, "Stick with me kid. I have a lot to teach you."

Thank you, Bob.

Random Thoughts and Ruminations of a Kid from Winona

- Early morning walks and lunches with Eddy Arnold
- Having a conversation with Mickey Gilley while sitting in the co-pilot's seat of his twin-engine plane – while he was flying it.
- Being introduced to Gene Autry. I was 46 years old and could only stammer, "Uh, uh, uh."
- Producing and directing a basketball game in Champaign, Illinois, on Christmas Eve when Kentucky and Illinois were

both among the top five teams in the national rankings. When we woke on the morning of the game the wind chill temperature was 80° below zero. My beard froze when I walked 20 feet from the hotel to the restaurant. It was so cold the referees weren't able to fly to Champaign, so they had to use high school officials. That was 1983. I'm sure my rental car is still frozen in the parking lot.
- Long conversations with Fred Foy, the legendary radio voice that implored us to "Return to those thrilling days of yesteryear. The Lone Ranger rides again!"
- Sitting with Les Paul in his home at 3 o'clock in the morning and talking about the multitrack recording console he invented – while the original one was just a few feet away.
- Chatting in the wheelhouse with a towboat captain at 4 a.m. as he explained how he was navigating his vessel to push a dozen barges up the Mississippi River without running aground in the darkened channel.
- Directing weekend Sports Center programs for ESPN just before the weekly ACC Basketball Game of the Week I was producing and directing.
- Michigan football coach Bo Schembechler grabbing himself in a very inappropriate place and yanking to show his displeasure to the referees…two seconds after I had cut to a live head-to-toe shot of him looking directly into the camera in a nationally televised game. My color analyst Lee Corso simply said, "Oops".
- Making Brenda Lee laugh when I told her I could say I loved her music when I was a kid and knowing it wouldn't

offend her since she was only a year older than I was when she had her first hits.
- Dinner with NBC News anchor David Brinkley and discussions with Walter Cronkite about a program he was going to host for me. Unfortunately, plans for the program had to be cancelled. I regret not having the chance to work with him.
- A husky 5-year-old, nicknamed "Moose," spitting out his milk during a live Romper Room commercial for a local dairy and yelling, "This s*** is sour!"
- Producing and hosting a live, three-hour international webcast for the United Methodist Church just 37 hours after 9/11. We had two guests in the studio, people in New York and Washington who had seen the planes hit and six pastors from Oklahoma City who had been involved in the aftermath of the Murrow Building bombing. We also had a missionary join us from Palestine, where it was 3 a.m. local time. We could hear gunfire in the background as she talked. Over 5,000 people logged in for the event. Another 6,000 listened to the program in the next few days. I had never done a webcast in my life and had to learn how while I was preparing it. Bob would have been proud.
- Having a deep discussion about history and philosophy with Laugh-In's Arte Johnson between takes. He was probably the smartest actor I ever worked with … and one of the nicest.
- Standing on stage next to the newly elected governor of Georgia as his supporters cheered on election night.
- Riding in a helicopter with Alabama governor Fob James on the way to an oil rig in the Gulf of Mexico and

muttering at him because I had to cut off my beard (federal regulation) to even get on the platform. He thought it was funny.
- Sportscaster Jack Eaton, the subject for another entire book. I miss that man.
- Interviewing a 109-year-old man. He couldn't remember what he had for breakfast, but he described in great detail the time he met President Roosevelt (Teddy, not Franklin). He also recounted the stories his father told him about fighting in the Civil War.
- Explaining to Dallas Cowboys quarterback Danny White and two very large linemen that they had arrived too late to appear on our live national telethon. They were going to sing, "Mamas Don't Let Your Babies Grow Up to be Cowboys," but we were near the end of the show, so they had no time to rehearse. The trio had just spent four turbulent hours in Danny's private plane as he dodged thunderstorms all the way between Dallas and Nashville. They were extremely gracious and fortunately did not use me as a practice dummy.
- Winning an Emmy Award for producing and directing The Big 10 Football and Basketball game of the week.
- Seeing Dallas star Victoria Principal walk into the studio at seven in the morning without make-up and wondering why I was even bothering to pay a makeup artist to be there.
- Laughing as Harry Morgan told story after story about "December Bride," "M*A*S*H," and his films and co-stars, pausing only to do another take.

- Sitting offstage as the director counted down the final 30 seconds before my first live network special. Could I do it? "Sure you can," Bob would have told me. So I did.
- Working with Elvis Presley's conductor Joe Gurcio, the musical director for a special I was producing.
- Garth Brooks standing in the edit bay with me and complimenting the work of my 12-year-old daughter in the network series I was producing and then surprising her with a call to tell her how good she was. Kristen went to school the next day and struggled to get classmates to believe her. "You won't believe what happened last night," she breathlessly told them. "Garth Brooks called me and told me he liked seeing me on TV." They finally believed her.
- Confiscating the napkin Steve Allen used to scribble notes as he prepared to present a Lifetime Achievement Award to Milton Berle on an awards show I was directing. "Overserved" host Burt Reynolds sulking because the production assistant assigned to him had rejected his amorous advances. She was my wife.
- Directing a video in the control center of a prison in Santa Fe, New Mexico. When I turned to my audio engineer and asked him to bring in a shotgun so we could shoot, the guard was apoplectic. "You can't bring a shotgun in here," he screamed. "Let me rephrase that," I told the audio man. "Please bring in the elongated, highly directional microphone so we can videotape in here." The guard was suspicious of us for the rest of the day.
- Looking out my hotel window as I watched Los Angeles burn all around me. I had arrived in LA on business that day, just a few hours before a jury handed down the verdict

that declared the five policemen who had beaten Rodney King were innocent. It was my third riot.
- Sitting strapped behind a 240-pound cameraman on top of a van driving 70mph down Interstate 40 to get a four-second shot for a promotional video. We made the 15-mile round trip three times. We were stupid.
- Handing a UPI bulletin to then Senate Minority Leader Howard Baker, a supporter of President Nixon during the Watergate scandal. This was Baker's first news of the infamous 18½ minute gap in a crucial White House recording. The senator grimaced, shook his head and told me, "If this is true, it's all over." It was, and it was.
- Standing in Times Square on New Year's Eve and watching the ball drop at midnight. We had just come out of a performance of Les Miserables and walked up to the edge of the crowd. The weather was perfect. After the ball dropped, we walked a block up the roped-off sidewalk to our hotel, where we went upstairs and opened the windows over Times Square to watch the rest of the festivities. All paid for by a client I was meeting with two days later.
- Talking with a young boy who sometimes accompanied his wrestler father Rocky Johnson to the TV studio for the Saturday morning matches I was directing. Little Dwayne grew up to be "The Rock."
- Sitting in the control room and preparing to videotape a program with Vice-President Spiro Agnew and telling a cameraman to, "Truck (move) farther left. I want to shoot the vice-president from there." Feeling a tap on my shoulder as a secret service agent politely, but firmly told

me, "Uh, we don't use the word 'shoot' around the vice president." He convinced me.

- Standing with Agnew and the owner of the Memphis Grizzlies pro football team a few hours later as we prepared to board the press elevator to the owner's suite to watch the game. The operator refused to allow Agnew on the elevator because he didn't have a press pass. After a prolonged discussion and the intervention of the stadium manager, the operator reluctantly agreed to allow the vice president to board the elevator. But as Agnew's secret service detail started to get on with him, the man put his hand on the first agent's chest and said, "Him [Agnew] I know. You I don't." The agent calmly pulled back his jacket, revealing his gun. "We go with the vice president." They did.

- Getting slugged and knocked through a swinging door during a live network television program by the manager of a big star because I refused to let his client go on the air in his severely impaired condition. I won't name the star. You would watch "The Jeffersons" reruns with a different perspective if I did.

- Having three good friends inducted into the Country Music Hall of Fame.

- Sitting 12th row center and having a conversation with my seatmate Carley Simon at the Grammy Awards…and then watching Paul Simon, Johnny Mathis, Barbra Streisand and many others perform. Before the show, Carley grabbed my shoulders as we all jumped to our feet and applauded an audience member walking down the aisle to his front row seat. "It's Roy Rogers, it's Roy Rogers," she gushed. Even the stars have their heroes.

Final Thoughts from Bryan

Bob (Mr. Chisholm) entered my life on October 25, 1958. It was the grand opening of radio station WONA in Winona, Mississippi. I was one of many people who crowded into that tiny studio for a celebration of the station's first day on the air.

I was 12 years old. To be honest, I don't remember Bob from that day. He was just one more entity among the blur of owners, officials, disc jockeys, music, commercials, hubbub and fanfare that made up the festivities. I vividly remember, however, the first time I *experienced* Bob Chisholm.

Sometime after the grand opening, I started hanging around the station. Bob and the announcers were always encouraging to me as I sought to learn as much as I could about radio. I was walking through the tiny office area one day after getting Cokes for a couple of announcers, one of my official volunteer duties.

Bob was sitting at his desk staring intently at a blank piece of paper nestled in the old manual typewriter he used to write his news stories. He was completely engrossed in what he was thinking and never noticed me standing there. Without warning, his hands exploded, and he furiously attacked that venerable old Underwood.

Words poured onto the page as his two index fingers pounded the keys at a furious pace that blurred his movement. His eyes never left the page as he sat hunched over the typewriter, a cigarette dangling carelessly from his lips.

He was creating a story, words he would soon speak over the airways, soon to have them vanish like the wisps of smoke that enveloped his head. Only, as I learned much later, often they did not vanish. Over the years, so many of those words lingered, some stinging consciences, others spreading enlightenment, information, sorrow or joy.

Some were harsh or angry. Some were soothing and calming. Many were unashamedly forward thinking. Often, they were amusing and thought provoking. Always, they were insightful, measured and well-reasoned. He was the ultimate journalist, a dedicated gatherer and disseminator of information and truth.

As suddenly as he had started, he paused and lifted his ever-present cup of black coffee to his lips, sipping the bitter brew that was so strong it almost had to be chiseled from the cup. Satisfied with what he had written, he set down his cup and smiled. He never looked up as I quietly walked through the room to deliver my bundle. At that moment I realized he was already what I wanted to be when I grew up.

Acknowledgements

This book would not have been possible without the amazing memories of Dr. Tom Dulin, Hank Holmes, Phyllis Townsend Ward and Bryan Cottingham, my co-author and friend since childhood. I could not have asked for a better writing partner.

Thanks also to those book lovers in my life, who encouraged and inspired me, among them Kat, William, Josh, Syl, Rozzy, Matthew, Betty, Suzanne, Chris, Donnie and Jim, our editor/publisher, who always made our writing better. A special thanks goes to the Special Collections Department at University Libraries, University of Memphis, for their help in gathering photos for this book.

—Candy Chisholm Justice

This book was not written in a vacuum. Many special people contributed to its completion.

My wife, Julie, who patiently (most of the time) listened to many of these stories over and over, until she finally said, "Why don't you put them in a book?" With her encouragement and support, here they are. A grateful thank you to Candy Chisholm Justice, who graciously invited me to be a part of this project.

Bob and Carole Graves, along with my brothers Joe and Jimmy Cottingham, lent their remembrances of growing up in a small town. Many of the photographs in this book came from the kindness of Steve Lester and the Bank of Winona staff, as well as Paula Hood McCaulla, Sue Stidham, and the late Bain Hughes.

Thank you to the *Winona Times* for allowing us into their archives to find news stories that stirred our imaginations and piqued our interest once again. Appreciation goes to Seth and Sharon Kent who have worked hard to continue WONA's service to Winona and the surrounding area while still remembering its legacy.

Longtime friends and colleagues Dr. Richard Ranta, Roxie Gee, and Ken Rees helped keep alive the shared memories of the career that followed WONA. Stanley Porter and Phil Slavick were guides who built on the foundation and continued mentorship of Bob Chisholm over the years. And the thousands of announcers, actors, producers, directors, engineers, and production crew members who lent their talents, support, and wisdom to help shape an exciting 50-year career in radio and television.

And especially, our editor Jim Dickerson who believed in our story and challenged us to be better writers.

To each of you, and so many more, "Thank you".

—Bryan Cottingham

RADIO GLOSSARY

-30-	An old newspaper marking that indicated the end of a story. Bob sometimes used this in his scripts.
AM	Amplitude Modulation. The frequency standard for early radio
AP	Associated Press. One of the two main news services that provided state, national and international news to local radio stations via teletype. See UPI
ASCAP	The American Society of Composers, Authors, and Publishers. One of the two largest music publishing companies. See BMI.
A Side	The side of a 45rpm record that featured the song record labels felt was likely to be the most popular.
B Side	A song on the opposite side of a 45rpm record from the featured song, often a "throwaway" song whose only purpose was to fill space. Record companies tried not to place two potentially popular songs on the same two-sided record. A double-sided hit meant buyers got two popular songs for the price of one. Sometimes the B side unexpectedly became the more popular song.
Board	The panel where the announcer sat and controlled records, audio tapes, and live announcements. See Tight Board.

BMI	Broadcast Music, Incorporated. The other major music publishing company. See ASCAP.
Cart	Short for cartridge. A rectangular audio tape player usually used for commercials or single music playback. It was faster and more convenient than early reel-to-reel audio tape.
Call letters	A unique four-digit set of letters that identifies a specific radio or TV station. Call letters are requested by a station and then approved by the FCC. Early stations can be identified by their three-digit call letters. In this country, stations with call letters that start with W are located east of the Mississippi, while those west of the river start with K. Some exceptions are made for stations that went on the air before the prefixes were designated.
C&W	Country and Western music, a format made popular in the 40s and 50s, later changed to Country Music.
Classical	Music featuring Symphony orchestras, played almost exclusively on public radio stations.
Clear Channel	High powered AM stations who were given exclusive rights to a frequency after dark. Because no other station's local signal interfered, the clear channel station could be heard over a large part of the country. Prominent clear channel stations included: WWL in New Orleans, Cincinnati's WLW, WSM radio in Nashville (The Grand Ole

Opry), and a personal favorite of young people, WLS in Chicago. Teenagers would lie under the covers each night with transistor radios and listen to the antics of Dick Bionde every week-night.

Control Room	The room that contained all the elements needed for a broadcast.
Copy	Written commercials or promotions to be read by announcers.
Cueing	Early turntables were extremely bulky, so it took a few revolutions to bring them up to speed after they were turned on. To prevent a record from "wowing", the DJ would set the needle in the groove between songs, spin it slowly until he heard the first sound and then spin it back a half revolution to prepare it for airing. See "Wowing"
Daytimer	A radio station that was only licensed to broadcast during daylight periods. The specific sign-on times for each day were designated by the FCC and strictly monitored.
Dead Air	A period of silence on the radio. It usually signaled the station was having technical difficulties or, more often, that the DJ was not paying attention. Dead air was one of the biggest fears of announcers.
DJ	Disc Jockey. A person who plays music and talks on the radio. A term first used in the late 50s to describe announcers who played Rock and Roll music.

Dollar a Holler	Term to describe low-cost radio commercials.
Doo Wop	A form of popular music in the 50s. It got its name from the sounds made by background singers.
EP	Extended Play. The name given to larger vinyl records containing programs, usually 15 minutes or 30 minutes in length.
FCC	Federal Communications Commission. First established in 1934 to regulate and oversee radio and (later) television stations. All stations feared the FCC because the agency had the sole right to grant and revoke lucrative broadcast licenses. See Chapter "The FCC Steps In."
Format	The style of a radio station, generally defined by the music it played. Later, this term expanded to include talk radio, sports radio, or forms that appealed to limited audiences.
FM	Frequency Modulation. A higher frequency standard that became popular in the 70s. This frequency produced a higher quality signal that also allowed the use of stereo.
Frequency	The measurement of radio waves, usually expressed in kilocycles or megacycles (Later kilohertz and megahertz). AM radio broadcasts between 550 and 1,600 kilohertz. FM broadcasts between 88 and 108 megahertz. Many stations identify themselves by their frequency in order to make it

	easier for listeners to find them on the radio dial (95.1 The Farm).
Log	A document that listed all programs, commercials, and other details of the broadcast. It was required by the FCC and was also used as a billing instrument for advertisers.
LP	Long playing album. Vinyl records that contained 6-8 songs on a side and played at a speed of 33⅓ rpm. These were the most common types of records played in the 50s and early 60s.
MC	Emcee – the host of a program or event
Meter Readings	Hourly measurements of a variety of electronic data from the transmitter. These were required by the FCC. Most announcers either hated taking readings or forgot to take them, often causing them to have to make up readings, a challenging exercise if the FCC showed up for surprise inspections.
Mic	Microphone
MOR	Middle of the Road. A music format often incorporated by small-town radio stations in order to please the largest number of listeners in the area. It included Big Band music, vocal harmonies, and such artists as Frankie Laine, Perry Como, Rosemary Clooney, and Tennessee Ernie Ford. In the 60s, some softer Rock and Roll songs were added.
Payola	The practice of paying disc jockeys to play certain songs, helping the record label to sell

	more records. The practice was abruptly stopped (or at least curtailed) in the early 60s when the scheme was exposed and exploded into a scandal that sent some prominent DJs to jail or ruined their career. The closest announcers came to payola in the small markets was to get an occasional free burger at the Satellite Drive-In.
Pot	Potentiometer. The round knob on an older control board that controls the volume. Later replaced by faders.
PSA	Public Service Announcement. "Commercials" for charities or organizations that operated in the public interest. PSAs were aired free on stations. For many years, stations were required to devote a portion of the broadcast day to items and announcements of interest to the public at large.
Pre-roll	Turning on a turntable one or two seconds before the song was put on air in order to bring the record up to speed. See Cue.
Ratings	A measurement of the number of people listening to a radio or television station in a given quarter hour. Ratings are used to determine advertising rates. A *Share* represents the percentage of listeners tuned in to a particular station. A *Rating* is based on the number of listeners compared to the entire available audience.
Reel-to-Reel	A tape recorder for recording and playing back music or spoken word. The recorder consisted of a playback reel that held the

	tape and a take-up reel that received and spooled the tape as it played.
Remote	A live broadcast originating away from the radio station, usually connected in the early years by a telephone line.
Rock and Roll	A musical form that originated in the early 50s. Rock and Roll was a blend of African-American music such as jazz, rhythm and blues, boogie-woogie, gospel, jump blues, as well as country music. Credit for the name goes to 50s Disk Jockey Alan Freed who coined the term on his hit radio program in Cleveland, Ohio.
RPM	Revolutions Per Minute. Records played at speeds of $33^{1/3}$, 45, or 78 rpms.
Station ID	Station Identification. Stations identify themselves frequently during the hour to make sure listeners know the station they are listening to (see ratings). Once an hour, near the top of each hour, stations are required to identify themselves by call letters and location (WONA, Winona Mississippi)
Slip cue	Holding a record still while the turntable spun beneath as the announcer was introducing a song. Used by DJs to bring a record up to speed more quickly.
Tickers	The nickname for teletype machines that provided news to radio stations. Also known as "Wires".
Tight Board	Airing the elements of a program close together, without dead air.

Top 40	A music format adopted in the mid-1960s. Stations would play a rotation of the top 40 rock and roll songs each week. The rotation would change on a weekly basis, dropping songs that had become less popular to make room for new releases.
Transcription	Programs prerecorded on larger vinyl records (EPs). In order to differentiate between recorded and live broadcasts, these programs were usually introduced by the phrase, "The following program is transcribed."
Transmitter	A tall tower, usually far from the radio station, that broadcasted the signal to listeners.
Turntable	Large circular platforms for records. Most radio stations positioned a 16" diameter turntable on each side of the control board. While a record was playing on the air on one turntable, the DJ would prepare, or cue the next record to be played. Most turntables offered three speed choices, $33\frac{1}{3}$ rpm for albums, 45rpm for single play records, and 78rpm for older (and larger) single records.
UPI	United Press International. One of the two main teletype services that provided state, national and international news to local radio stations. See AP
Vinyls	Records made from vinyl acetate. The predecessors of CDs.
VU Meter	Volume Unit indicator. The meter on the control board that showed voice, music, and

	tape volume being broadcast. The ideal volume level was 85 percent-100 percent.
Wowing	Putting a record on the air before it was fully up to speed, resulting in the artist starting out singing in slow motion.

BIBLIOGRAPHY

Davis, Janel. "Fannie Lou Hamer: sick and tired sharecropper became political force," *Atlanta Journal Constitution.*

Demuth, Jerry. "Fannie Lou Hamer: Tired of Being Sick and Tired!" *The Nation*, June 1964.

Rowland, Dunbar. *The Official and Statistical Register of the State of Mississippi (1924-1928).* J.J. Little and Ives Company, New York, 1927.

Spruill, Marjorie and Jesse Spruill Wheeler. "Woman suffrage Movement begins," *Mississippi History Now*, December 2001.

Milton Keynes UK
Ingram Content Group UK Ltd.
UKHW021359011124
450401UK00032B/234/J